FLIPPING SCHOOLS!

WHY IT'S TIME TO TURN YOUR SCHOOL AND COMMUNITY INSIDE OUT

MALCOLM GROVES AND
JOHN WEST-BURNHAM

First Published 2020

by John Catt Educational Ltd,
15 Riduna Park, Station Road,
Melton, Woodbridge IP12 1QT

Tel: +44 (0) 1394 389850
Email: enquiries@johncatt.com
Website: www.johncatt.com

ISBN: 978 1 912 906 66 6

Set and designed by John Catt Educational Limited

Table of Contents

LIST OF FIGURES

LIST OF TABLES

Introduction: Why We Wrote This Book

Schools can be extremely exasperating! Many do achieve wonderful things for and with their students. But it seems to us this often happens in spite of the way they are organised and in spite of the way the system holds them to account.

We think it is possible to do even better by thinking differently. Our belief, supported by a wide range of evidence, is that this involves flipping the mindset away from seeing the school as an organisation towards viewing it as a community. It involves turning school-centric thinking inside out to open up a community-centred and learner-focused mindset. That change and its rationale, implications and practicality is what this book is about.

The origins of this book lie in a question. Well, two questions actually. Both were posed to us by Charles Fadel, a global education thought leader and founder of the Center for Curriculum Redesign in Boston, Massachusetts. He had just read our book *Leadership for Tomorrow* (Groves et al. 2017). In it we argued the need for fresh thinking about schooling, notably in regard to the way purpose and quality are understood. We suggested that, as a result, some current assumptions about school improvement need to be revisited.

In particular, we highlighted the accumulation of evidence that suggests between only 20% and 30% of the factors that influence educational outcomes are directly within the school's control. We concluded that we therefore need to encourage schools to pay a little more attention to those social, economic and environmental factors beyond the school's gates, and seek to exert some greater influence over them than is currently the case if we are to secure the best futures for all young people.

If that is correct, Charles asked us, what is the right balance between focusing our attention on curriculum reform and trying to influence external factors? We responded that the curriculum, and indeed everything else about a school that is bound up within that 20–30%, is fundamentally important, and we absolutely must do the best possible job we can with this for the sake of all our young people. Our point was rather that, while curriculum reform is necessary to do the best possible job with everything within the school's power, it is not sufficient to take us beyond the horizon to the next stage of school improvement.

But Charles then had a second, more pointed, question. In that case, he asked, what is it that a school which is looking to work on the 70–80% area as well actually does differently? This book is our attempt to answer that question.

Many of the factors at work beyond the school which influence educational outcomes are of course subject to wider political and social forces. A school is not able to engage in structural social or economic change, nor should it attempt to do so. But we also believe that those who argue that schools should only concentrate on what happens within their walls, and over which they have direct control, are misguided. We believe there is, between these two extremes, a legitimate community dimension in which all schools have a part to play.

Over the last decade, since 2010 in England at least, this is a view that has been pretty unfashionable, to put it mildly. Previous decades, stretching back to the 1920s, had seen the development of both strong theoretical arguments and practical initiatives which explored the community involvement of schools from a range of perspectives. Often these initiatives, spearheaded in pioneering local authorities such as Cambridgeshire or Leicestershire, took the form of programmes that established new 'community schools', which then usually required some capital investment to create additional facilities for community use.

One early such visionary, Henry Morris, described the aspiration in these terms:

> As the community centre of the neighbourhood the village college would provide for the whole man, and abolish the duality of education and ordinary life. It would not only be the training ground for the art of living, but the place in which life is lived, the environment of a genuine corporate life. The dismal dispute of vocational and non-vocational education would not arise in it. It would be a visible demonstration in stone of the continuity and never-ceasingness of education. There would be no 'leaving school' – the child would enter at three and leave the college only in extreme old age! (Morris 1924, section XIV)

Morris continued:

> [The village college] would have the virtue of being local so that it would enhance the quality of actual life as it is lived from day to day – the supreme object of education ... It would not be divorced from the normal environment of those who would frequent it from day to day, or from that great educational institution, the family ... The village college could lie athwart the daily lives of the community it served; and, in it, the conditions would be realised under which education would not be an escape from reality, but an enrichment and transformation of it.

The New Labour government of 1997 took some of this thinking to heart as it introduced a community dimension to its specialist school programme, intended to make specialist educational facilities and resources more widely available between and beyond schools. It also developed a programme of 'extended schools' to 'provide a range of services and activities, often beyond the school day, to help meet the needs of its pupils, their families and the wider community' (DfES 2005, p.7).

By 2008, Cabinet Office minister Liam Byrne was even saying in an interview with *The Guardian*:

> In the medieval days we built communities around the manor house, then in the 19th century we built communities about the factory, and in the 21st century we need to build communities around schools ... we have not just an education service for the kids,

> but on that same site we need family learning services because a lot of parents may not be in work and may need re-equipping with new skills to get back into work. There may be a need for a different kind of health service that is co-located in schools with a bigger emphasis on children and adult mental health services. (Byrne 2008)

The support provided in England by both local and central government for such development, whether in terms of policy or funding, simply withered away in the subsequent ten years. Where the work continued, usually at a reduced level, it was often through the hard work of dedicated enthusiasts, frequently drawing on local strengths inherited from the achievement of previous generations. Vital as that has been, it is time to make afresh the argument for the community engagement of all schools against the backdrop of a hugely different and now highly fragmented system of school provision.

Our argument will be that education in England in particular, but maybe not just in this country alone, has in recent years arrived at the end of a cul-de-sac from which we now need to escape. In this case, though, getting out of the cul-de-sac does not mean going back to the point from which we turned off into it. It means finding a way to pick up the main highway again at a different point, one where it is possible to learn both from all that went before and from all that has happened since.

The crucial difference we are suggesting is that new thinking about community engagement and schools is no longer focused primarily on providing additional facilities for wider community use. Instead it begins from a premise of securing better learning outcomes for children and young people as its core purpose. Its key drivers are building social capital and securing social equity. It is about social justice, not simply social mobility.

This does not necessarily require capital investment, welcome as that may undoubtedly be in many situations. Nor does it require some type of formal designation for a school. Rather it is about the nature of the school as a community, and the quality of relationships a school builds, fosters and reflects outwards at every level. It therefore holds the opportunity for every school, not just some.

In examining this possibility further, we will argue in Part One that our present thinking about school improvement is no longer having a significant effect in terms of addressing the performance gaps that exist and may even now be taking us backwards because of some inherent design weaknesses. In Part Two, we will look at the evidence for the impact of poverty, social class and genetic inheritance on educational achievement. We will consider the changes that have taken place in the nature of families and of childhood, as well as in our understanding of community.

Taken together, all of these factors will help to explain why change is now necessary, as well as offering some clues to the nature of that change. They will lead us to what we believe is the key to the next stage of improvement, the building of social capital. We will explore its implications for schools, and in doing so we will identify four building blocks of change, derived from the nature of social capital, that we think now need real focus in order to shape a different future for schools in very constrained times (see Figure 1).

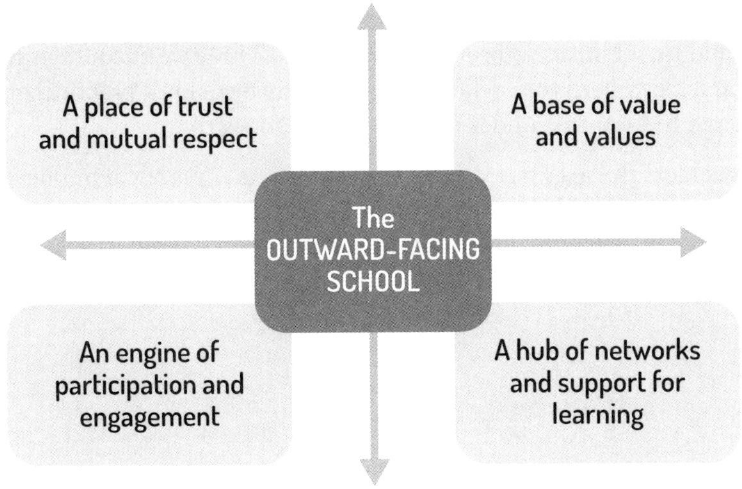

Figure 1: The Four Building Blocks of Change

In Part Three, we will look at each of these building blocks in turn, seeking to explore the educational principles underpinning them. Firstly, we will talk about a person-centred school, based on trust and mutual respect. Such a school begins by modelling community in its own organisation and daily living through a clear focus on the quality of relationships at every level. Secondly, we will consider the implications of those values for the curriculum. Thirdly, we will seek to develop a greater understanding of the nature and importance of stakeholder engagement in schools and how to remove barriers to it being effective. Finally in Part Three, we will explore the connected and collaborative leadership that is needed to bring about such change and to escape the present school improvement cul-de-sac.

We will look at how the four building blocks are emerging in practice in four schools today. We will tease out eight wider lessons from the experience of those schools that may help others to move forward, and we will offer a few possible tools and strategies that may help schools wanting to think about applying those lessons to their own practice and development.

Taken together, the four building blocks can help you to flip your school over and turn it inside out. At the end of Part Three we encourage you to take stock of where your school is at currently by using a practical online tool, and to keep this under review moving forward.

To conclude, in Part Four we will look at the wider practical implications of this thinking and this direction of travel for school leaders, as well as for system leadership and education policy.

PART ONE
Why Change Is Needed

1. A Germ of An Idea

Change is always inevitable, but positive change requires both intention and purpose. In this book we aim to set out a basis for positive change in the school system, both in England, which has chosen its own idiosyncratic path at this time, but also perhaps more widely. We will argue that now is the time to re-think and re-interpret some of the underlying premises of what our schools currently do. We are not thinking here so much about how schools are structured and organised. (Schools in England may feel they have had more than enough of that in recent years with limited benefit.) Rather we are talking about the real purpose of schools and how well they achieve that.

Although our starting point is the English school system, we believe our ideas may be of much wider relevance to schools globally. This is because the root of the problem lies in what Pasi Sahlberg has called GERM – the Global Education Reform Movement – which in many countries has led to increased competition, greater choice, stronger accountability, and a heavy reliance on standardised testing.

We suggest change is necessary because what we are currently doing in England as a result of GERM is no longer achieving all that the movement set out to accomplish in terms of equity and opportunity for all. A focus on school improvement through GERM over something like a quarter of a century has achieved some worthwhile progress, but we believe the inevitable first signs of stalling and eventual decline have been evident for a while (see chapter 2 for more on this). We have reached that stage in the life cycle of school improvement where more of the same will become increasingly unproductive.

This relates to the phenomenon of the sigmoid curve, developed by Charles Handy to represent a new life cycle emerging from an existing one. Handy's insight is that individuals, organisations and systems must understand where they are in terms of their present life cycle and then, at the right moment, plan and implement transformational change. Act too soon and you lose the benefits of the present cycle. However, act too late and you are heading downhill, and it becomes too late to turn things round.

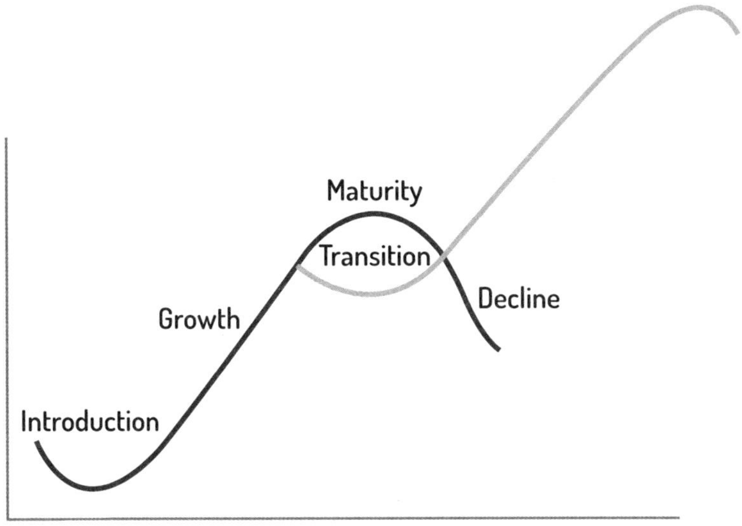

Figure 2: The Change Life Cycle – Charles Handy's Sigmoid Curve

Our contention is that now is the time for the English education system in particular to start to focus its attention on carving out a new life cycle. Furthermore, we suggest it is necessary to think and act differently in this new life cycle. This means moving away from purely school-centric thinking to more effectively influencing the environment and community in which a school exists. That is the essence of what we mean when we speak of flipping the school and its communities inside out.

Of course, the problem with the image of the sigmoid curve is that it suggests change happens in a linear fashion (even if the lines are curved!). This may be a necessary visual simplification for explanatory purposes, but it is deeply misleading to think that there is one clear, straightforward route forward.

We know that those of you who are persuaded by what we have to say would probably much prefer it if we could offer you some magic formula; a handbook with, say, ten simple steps to achieving our vision. So, let us be straight at the outset. We do not think life is like that. Change is in fact unclear, uneven, messy, and always subject to experimentation and failure. We have, however, reflected on the experience of four actual schools and their leaders, and in Part Three we draw out some broad lessons from their practice which may serve as a starting point to help inform the journeys of others, while in Part 4 we consider some of the implications for school and system leaders.

With that really important proviso, we aim to present a range of evidence – combining research, theory and professional reflection, but also rooted in clear values and grounded in practice – to suggest a basis on which schools individually as well as collectively could start to initiate and explore positive change.

We hope all this in turn can help in understanding more clearly the shape of the next phase of improvement and perhaps lead to fresh systemic development. But before that, it is necessary first to look at where we are now and understand a little more about how exactly we came to be here.

2. The End of the Road for School Improvement

The evidence that school improvement in England is stalling has been accumulating for some time. The average science, mathematics and reading scores of pupils in England have not changed between 2006 and 2016 (Jerrim and Shure 2016, p.4). Moreover, the attainment gap between secondary students who receive free school meals and those who do not (28 percentage points) has hardly budged in that decade. Thousands of poor children who are in the top 10% nationally at age 11 do not make it into the top 25% five years later (Wilshaw 2016). Yet at the same time, and despite this overall static picture, the number of schools rated 'good' or 'outstanding' increased to 89% of all schools in 2017 (Ofsted 2018).

The need for an alternative perspective on school improvement is further reinforced by the implications of these recent findings from the Education Policy Institute:

> Over the same period (2007–2016), the [disadvantage] gap by the end of primary school narrowed by 2.8 months, and the gap by age 5 narrowed by 1.2 months. At current trends, we estimate that it would take around 50 years for the disadvantage gap to close completely by the time pupils take their GCSEs. (Andrews et al. 2017, p.6)

So unless something changes, progress in securing better education outcomes for all appears to be pretty much stuck. Indeed, in summer 2019, the Education Policy Institute amended their estimate of the time needed to close the gap in England at current rates of progress to 500 years (Hutchinson et al. 2019, p.11).

Schools did not arrive in this present cul-de-sac by accident. Equally they did not set off down this road with malign intent, even though we all perhaps chose to ignore some important warning signs along the way. At its root, this journey began with a legitimate desire for schools to be accountable. The problem lies in misunderstanding to whom and for what should schools be accountable, as well as the way that accountability should be achieved. Because accountability drives behaviour, we must begin by understanding how it has become a problem in order to begin to see how we can change what we do.

What do we mean by accountability?

For our purposes here, we are more than content to adopt the view taken by the National Foundation for Educational Research in their 2018 literature review of the topic. Accountability is at root 'the practice of holding educational systems responsible for the quality of their products – students' knowledge, skills and behaviours' (NFER 2018, p.1). Other forms of accountability (such as financial integrity), though important, are secondary to this overarching purpose.

However, we would perhaps make a couple of clarifications to this definition. The first is to make clear that quality includes quality improvement as a process as well as an outcome. The two are interlinked. The second would be to make clear that the drive for accountability is about the responsibility of schools individually as well as the school system collectively. Both need to be able to demonstrate the quality of their outcomes while also demonstrating improvement in those outcomes over time.

For some years, the legitimate aspiration of UK governments for school improvement, and to hold schools to account for this, has been enshrined in the phrase 'the self-improving system'. Sometimes this has been extended into 'the self-improving school-led system'. In 2010, the Department for Education white paper *The Importance of Teaching* put it thus:

> The primary responsibility for improvement rests with schools ... the attempt to secure automatic compliance with [government]

> priorities reduces the capacity of the system to improve itself. Instead our aim should be to create a school system which is more effectively self-improving. (DfE 2010, p.13)

Greany and Higham (2018) trace the start of such thinking, as far as the UK government is concerned, to a 2006 Cabinet Office paper on public service reform (although this encapsulated ideas developed globally over a period of time). The paper describes a self-improving system as one in which 'incentives for continuous improvement and innovation are embedded within it' (Prime Minister's Strategy Unit 2006, p.4).

The idea of a 'self-improving system' was a response to the perceived failure of previous reform initiatives in the public sector, and crucially rested on the interaction of four key drivers to make it work (see Figure 3):

- Pressure from the government – with top-down performance management through stretching targets, regulation, inspection and direct intervention.
- Competitive provision – with market incentives to create competition between 'providers' and contestability over who provides public services.
- Pressure from citizens – with 'users' shaping services though voice and choice (and funding following user choices).
- Measures to build the capability and capacity of civil and public servants – through leadership and workforce reform, and the promotion of 'best practice' through funding dissemination and incentivising collaboration.

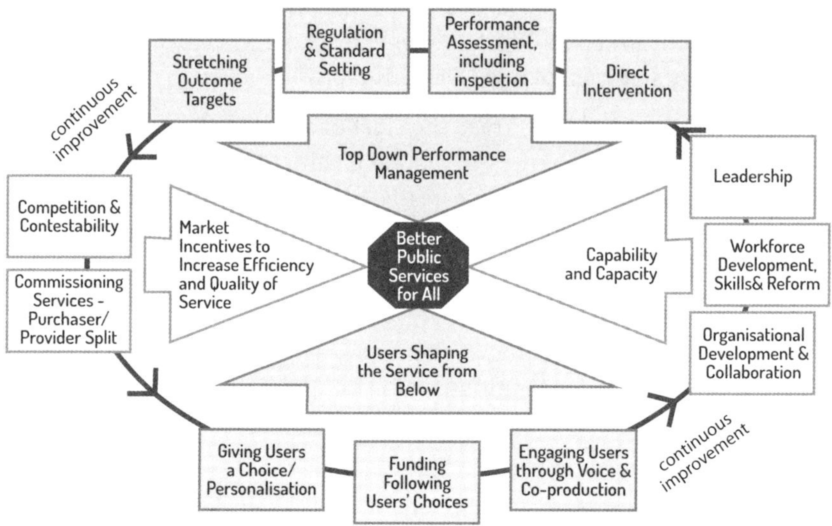

Figure 3: The UK Government's Approach to Public Service Reform (Prime Minister's Strategy Unit 2006, p.6)

The balance of these drivers shifted notably with a change of UK government in 2010. In the school system, much greater emphasis was given to top-down performance management. This led to a sharper range of narrower outcome measures, a tighter inspection regime, and the encouragement of a range of new school providers.

At the same time, comparatively little weight has been given to users shaping the service from below, except through one-off consumer purchasing decisions, while increased competition between schools has arguably created unresolved tensions in developing collective capacity across schools.

However, even if the model was operating optimally, the notion of a self-improving school system still poses a number of difficulties and misunderstandings, each of which has helped to lead to where we are now. (Of course, many of these difficulties also exist in other school improvement models, as well as applying to other areas of public service, such as healthcare.) We will look at these difficulties in a bit more detail below.

Difficulty 1: Who are the users?

If I buy a consumer item – let's say a car – it is fairly clear who the user will be. It might be me; it might be my friends or family. I might conceivably be buying on behalf of someone else, such as a company or a friend. But in any of these cases it is fairly straightforward for both the producer and the seller to know who to approach to get feedback on the product and to find out how well the product is meeting its users' needs.

Sometimes people do buy the wrong car for their purposes. For example, they buy a diesel car when a petrol one may be more appropriate for their journeys, or they buy one which does not have enough space for their needs. When that happens, it is a relatively straightforward matter to change it for a different car, even though there may be significant financial costs for doing so.

In England, our present school system too easily assumes this is an analogy which can be transferred across to choosing a school, and in this analogy the primary purchaser is seen as the parent or carer. National accountability measures, taking the form of data reflecting measurable test outcomes for pupils (as well as external inspection reports), are converted into league tables without much in the way of contextualisation. These are predicated on promoting and supporting the right of parents and carers to select the school they want for their child.

The assumption is that a consumer who is unhappy with their choice will either complain or choose to 'purchase' elsewhere. That assumes of course it is not too late to do so. But even if time permits, in many situations choosing a different school is far from a viable option, for reasons as varied as distance, travel, school capacity and friendships.

Yet the parent or carer is not the only 'user' of a school. It is a much more complicated picture, where in reality there are many different individuals and groups with an interest in schools and what they produce.

What about the child or young person who is benefiting from an education? What of the employer who seeks to draw on the 'outputs' of the school? Or whoever is paying the bill? And does the latter refer to the government alone or the wider taxpayer? In addition, the role of parent or carer is itself much more than that of simple consumer. They are in fact co-producers or co-educators who contribute directly to the final outcomes.

The essential point here is that the notion of accountability involves a much more complicated relationship than a simple market-based purchaser/consumer choice model would allow. Mechanisms of accountability need to reflect this complexity of relationships, as well as understand the nature of those relationships. We shall explore the nature of school community relationships further in Part Three.

Difficulty 2: What outcomes do different users want?

This multiplicity of users would perhaps matter less if it was clear they all had the same expectations. But is that in fact the case? Do they even know what each other wants? And if there are differences, can they be reconciled?

Everything we know tells us there is no natural consensus around desired outcomes. Not even educators agree. Education remains, to quote Gallie's phrase, an 'essentially contested concept' (Gallie 1955), for cutting across the legitimate and varied interests of all those different stakeholder groups lie deep philosophical divides. Guy Claxton and Bill Lucas (2015) characterise this split as being between three broad tribes, which they term 'roms', 'trads' and 'mods'.

The romantics (roms) are so-called because of their belief in the innate goodness of children who, by virtue of this innate quality, have no need for didactic teaching or adult authority. The traditionalists (trads), on the other hand, are so-called due to their view that teachers are respected sources of culturally important, tried-and-tested factual knowledge, which they pass on to children and then test through formal examination. Across both of these groups lies a spectrum of different emphases and views about the content and process of education. A third group, the moderates (mods), rejects this simplistic duality, understands complexity and knows there are no quick fixes, and so explores and tinkers in order to gain better understanding.

The point is that the individual school, as well as the system as a whole, has to navigate a path between these competing views. It does not follow that every stakeholder claim is of equal value, and the balance between them may well shift for different ages and stages of learning. Choices will have to be made, but both the school and the system needs to do this on the basis of clear values and a strong ethical compass. These values also need to be explicit so they are widely understood and, as far as possible, widely shared, even if the resulting decisions which flow from them remain contentious to some.

Schools are not necessarily unique in this regard. Thomas Maak, for example, argues that business leaders have to deal with moral complexity resulting from a multitude of stakeholder claims, and must endeavour to build enduring and mutually beneficial relationships with all relevant stakeholders. This he terms 'responsible leadership' (Maak 2007, p.331).[1] He goes on to describe the responsible business leader as 'a weaver of stakeholder relationships and as broker of social capital in pursuit of responsible change' (Maak 2007, p.340). But he could equally be describing a school leader, and we shall return to this in chapter 14.

In education, where different stakeholder claims potentially lead to different outcomes, any uniform pattern of accountability between schools that does not recognise the interaction of countervailing forces and local contexts will have real problems. We will explore the outcome-related elements of this dilemma further in chapter 12 and the stakeholder-related elements in chapter 13.

Difficulty 3: How does anyone know which schools are successful?

We have just noted that definitions of school success are not universally agreed by all those who have a legitimate interest in securing it. This will clearly impact on anyone's ability to come to a view as to whether success is in fact being achieved. But if we assume for a moment that there is a widely shared and agreed understanding of what success for any school looks like, another range of issues immediately open up before us.

1. 'Key to responsible leadership is the ability to enable and broker sustainable, mutual, beneficial relationships with stakeholders, to create stakeholder goodwill and trust, and ultimately a trusted business in society.'

In particular, while judging success clearly has to rest on more than just gut instinct (even though there may be a place for a 'sound nose', such as an experienced school inspector can possess), it is all too easy to be seduced into the trap of measurement. In this trap, what is important and of value, and what can be readily measured, become intertwined and end up in a tangle.

Stephen Gorard made this point (which has only grown in significance in the intervening years) when he wrote in 2009 that:

> School effectiveness is associated with a narrow understanding of what education is for. It encourages, unwittingly, an emphasis on assessment and test scores – and teaching to the test – because over time we tend to get the system we measure for and so privilege. (Gorard 2009, p.759)

The problem here does not lie with the notion of tests themselves. Their diagnostic value is clear for the learner, the school and the system. Nor, though we are easily seduced by it, does the problem lie with the notion of measurement per se. Measurement can be incredibly valuable and an important tool in asking powerful questions about performance. The problem lies with the way tests are used in terms of high-stakes accountability for schools, and the fact that in many respects the tests used as the basis for such accountability are really not fit for that purpose. The resulting measurements easily become skewed and error-strewn, and so can be confusing or misleading for users. This especially seems to be the case when measurements are used by politicians, as evidenced in the all too frequent (albeit logically impossible) demand that all schools should be above average.

We shall explore the practical and policy implications of this further in Part Four.

Difficulty 4: How do we recognise influences beyond the control of the school?

The fourth and final difficulty in current understandings of school accountability lies in the established knowledge that, while of course schools make a difference to educational outcomes, and 'good' schools make a still greater difference, there are factors which are not in the control of any school that make an even greater difference. Wilkinson and Pickett convincingly summarise the evidence that:

> Although good schools make a difference, the biggest influence on educational attainment, how well a child performs in school and later in higher education, is family background. (Wilkinson and Pickett 2010, p.103)

Stephen Gorard agrees with this, concluding that 'pupil prior attainment and background explain the vast majority of variation in school outcomes', while noting at the same time that this knowledge is 'now largely unremarked by academics and unused by policy-makers' (Gorard 2009, p.761).

It is perhaps ironic that most policies and strategies for improving educational outcomes have concentrated almost exclusively on improving the school, when we have known for some time that only at most 30% of the explanation for variations in school achievement appears to be attributable to factors within the school (see Moreno 2007, p.8). We will undertake a more in-depth analysis of this crucial issue in Part Two.

So, the system is set up to fail. The astonishing thing really is that so many schools do so well at overcoming this. But it would seem logical that the elements beyond the school, disproportionately significant in quantitative terms, should be accorded greater weight than currently recognised in practice. In essence, rather than focusing solely on school improvement for the last decade, perhaps we should have focused more attention on family and community improvement in order to achieve the educational outcomes we have been seeking.

In order to redress this imbalance, we urgently need to understand a little more about the contribution and interaction of the factors beyond the school that shape educational success. And this will be the theme of the next part of this book.

But before turning to that, let's take a moment to remind ourselves that if you believe, as we do, that accountability is important, it does not have to be done in anything like the way in which schools are currently being driven. There are other, very different ways of managing accountability, notably in the business world, which education and public services have often been enjoined to emulate and on which much of the current high-stakes accountability climate falsely claims to be based. This will be the subject of our next chapter.

3. A Glimpse of A Difference: Re-Imagining Accountability

It does not have to be this way. Consider an organisation which has no organisational chart, no staff meetings, no development plan, no key performance indicators, no formal budget, no staff manual, and where the biggest leadership focus is to support staff wellbeing. When judged against what is considered to be effective practice in most schools in the UK today, how could it possibly do well in (let alone survive) an Ofsted inspection?

The company we have described here is Timpson, based in Manchester. They claim to be the UK's fastest growing specialist locksmith service and describe themselves as 'the UK and Ireland's leading retail service provider of shoe repairs, key cutting, watch repairs, engraved personalised gifts, dry cleaning and assisted photo ID'. Timpson is characterised above all by a distinctive management ethos which it describes as follows:

> The Timpson ethos is to provide great customer service and to do this we operate an 'Upside Down' management style. We believe the best way to give great customer service is to give freedom to the colleagues that serve customers. (Timpson website)

Timpson, a family-owned business, has operated in this way for over 20 years, and its philosophy has evolved and developed in that time. At the same time the business has prospered, growing from 200 stores to over 2000, while profits have risen from £500,000 to £12 million.

The change began when the current chairman, Sir John Timpson, secured control of the business through a management buy-out and recognised that the only way the business would survive and succeed against much bigger and better-resourced competitors was to focus completely on offering outstanding customer service.

John's insight was that he could not achieve this by telling people what to do. It could only be achieved by fully empowering the staff who were providing that service to do so in the way they thought best for their customers. This meant turning the whole management structure of the company upside down. The role of management at every level had to become about supporting their team to do what they believed was right for customer-facing staff and their customers.

For several years, the new approach struggled. The problem, John said when interviewed by us for this book, was his area managers: 'They interfered! They could not see how they could be responsible for store performance if they were not telling people what to do.'[2] He continued:

> I had to persuade them to move from telling people to supporting people. Their job is about helping people develop. Leadership for me is all about looking after the people who look after the customers.

Staff are known as 'colleagues' and John explained that there are just two rules they must follow:

> They have to look the part and they have to put money in the till. We don't have any other rule book or set of procedures, we don't have any KPIs, we don't do any budgets, although we do look at income against last year.

Colleagues can set their own prices because no two jobs are the same. They are able to spend up to £500 on their own initiative to settle any complaint. Tills are not connected electronically to Timpson House at the centre, which is pointedly not known as the head office.

In general, John thinks that maybe 3% of colleagues at some time abuse this system and take money from the till, but believes he gets far more from the other 97% than if he tried to set up systems to prevent that relatively low level of fraud. The figures are all the more surprising

2. All quotes from Sir John Timpson are drawn from an interview with one of the authors 13.3.19.

given that, as a company policy now, about 10% of the workforce are ex-offenders, recruited directly from prisons.

The situation may also be helped by the strong focus the company places on promoting colleague wellbeing. For example, Timpson offers support (including financial help) at times of personal difficulty such as bereavement or debt, and it maintains holiday homes which are available to colleagues, all of whom get their birthday off each year.

There are a number of benefits to this upside-down approach to management. John says it makes the company very easy to run, and cites in particular:

- High levels of customer satisfaction.
- High levels of job satisfaction – with low levels of turnover or absenteeism – due to the increased wellbeing of staff.
- Lower management costs due to the inherent efficiencies in the approach. For example, the company has no marketing department ('everyone does marketing'), no departmental budgets, no compliance department, only two health and safety officers and, compared with most organisations of that size, very few meetings.

However, there are certain key ingredients that are necessary for the approach to succeed, as John explained:

> You absolutely have to have the right people and you have to be very good at saying goodbye to people for whom it turns out not to be the right thing.

Colleagues are recruited for their personality rather than their qualifications. The interview assessment is about them as a person and the way they present themselves, followed by working in a shop for half a day. All colleagues begin in this way and all promotions are internal.

The company invests heavily in colleague development. This begins with a 'new starter' course for all, but the company is also planning to open its own university to offer staff degree-level courses in upside-down management. A lot of training also happens through informal networking and sharing of ideas, help through WhatsApp groups, and the first-hand contact and encouragement of area managers and their small teams.

The most essential ingredient for John is commitment from the top:

> The CEO must be absolutely dedicated to this and set the example. It's all about getting the culture right.

Could upside-down management work in schools? It is certainly true that schools are in many respects more complex entities than privately owned companies. A school's customers are, as we have noted, more diverse, not so clearly defined, and come with competing expectations. Schools are not solely able to determine their outcomes and they face an inescapable level of external accountability. So, are there any lessons that can be learnt to help inform our thinking?

If you look back to our description of a company which has no organisational chart, no staff meetings, no development plan, no key performance indicators, no formal budget, no staff manual, and where the biggest leadership focus is to support wellbeing, it feels like a pretty radical step.

We shall return to this question later, but we need to state at the outset that we believe the answer is yes, we can do things differently, and such change must begin with school leaders. That is because in a school culture, relationships and wellbeing are key (as they are for Timpson), and these are directly within the control of every school leader.

As we shall see later from examples of English schools making these changes today, it does not require anyone's permission for school leaders, governors or trust boards to get started, though it does require courage and vision. But the more leaders who feel encouraged to take some first steps, recognising that (as Sir John Timpson stressed) it is the commitment of the leader that is vital, the less lonely it will be and the easier it will be to start to put high-stakes accountability back into its proper place and perspective.

Upside-down management thinking is, we suggest, part and parcel of turning the school inside out. This in turn means flipping from a school-centric mindset to a community-centred, learner-focused mindset.

Getting that right is the school equivalent of Timpson providing exceptional customer service.

Flipping the school mindset in this way requires building a different relationship with all stakeholders, including students, and focusing on removing barriers to learning. But it also requires a deeper understanding of the complex factors that influence educational achievement. This forms the theme of Part Two.

PART TWO

Why School-centric Thinking Isn't Enough Any More

4. The (Over-)Formalisation of Learning

In Part Two, we will consider the inter-relationship of three spheres of influence that can affect anyone's educational success, to help us understand what's gone missing on the present school-improvement journey. Our central hypothesis is that in England, as indeed in many other countries, we have viewed educational success largely in terms of the outcomes of schooling alone. As a result, we have not paid sufficient attention – either in our practice or in the mechanisms of accountability we have devised – to the influence of key contextual social factors, particularly family and parenting, community, poverty and social class. These all play a significant positive or negative role in the educational success of the most potent variable of all: the individual learner.

In saying that, let us be clear at the outset that this is not deficit thinking. It is not about making excuses for poor achievement because of the impoverished circumstances of many communities when the school could and should be doing better. It is about properly recognising, and taking proactive action around, the factors outside a school that affect what happens inside.

In recent years, education has become almost completely school-centric and, as a result, increasingly institutionalised, formalised and bureaucratised. Educational reform has thus been focused on school improvement, and this in turn has led to an excessive focus on internal structural change rather than acknowledging the proper significance of wider contextual factors.

When government policy in England has recognised such factors, it has usually been accompanied by initiatives with a very short life expectancy and compromised support. Every Child Matters, Sure Start and Children's Centres, for example, have all fallen victim to changes in policy, budget cuts or being given insufficient time to demonstrate their true potential.

Then there was the debate during the period of the New Labour government around the extended or full-service school, which in reality required both a fundamental reorientation of the nature of the school and its engagement with the community, as well as appropriate staffing and resourcing. Schools were not, and are not, designed or staffed to engage with wider social issues, and this seriously compromises their ability to make a significant and enduring impact when it comes to ameliorating disadvantage and securing equity.

But acknowledging this, of course, begs the question as to where the legitimate boundaries of a school's engagement and responsibility lie. We will seek to demonstrate how securing educational success for all does require a focus on social improvement rather than just school improvement alone. And, while the school is not the only or even lead agency in that, it does nonetheless have a crucial part to play.

The lack of a long-term strategic perspective in government education policy was commented on by the House of Commons Education Committee in their 2019 report:

> When we explored the issue of long-term planning in our inquiry, there were concerns that 'initiative-itis' was standing in for long-term vision. Indeed, we were not always able to discern overarching strategic objectives or funding prioritisation behind the Department's policy announcements, which have in recent months included online activity passports encouraging outdoor pursuits; free learning apps; tackling plastic waste; academisation; reducing teacher workload; life-saving classes in all schools; and improving teacher productivity through better technology use. (House of Commons Education Committee 2019, p.41)

Between January and April 2019, the committee's report identified nine quite distinct strategies at a total cost of £1093.8m, but notes that:

> Whilst these initiatives were doubtless important and beneficial, we were concerned that this busy schedule masked a wider absence of engagement around what the 5–19 education sector could and should look like in future.

Central to any discussion of the problems with the dominant school improvement-based approach is our concern at the lack of coherence in identifying the core business of education, as well as the failure to think strategically about it. Improvement has come to mean short-term, disjointed incrementalism, manifested in piecemeal interventions that are essentially diversions. For example, Joanna Williams, in a recent Policy Exchange paper (Williams 2019, p.7), identifies six future policy reform areas for education, of which three are directly related to the school system:

- Raise standards in schools through a commitment to improving behaviour in the classroom, and prioritising the expectation and enforcement of high standards of discipline within all schools.
- Improve teaching by cutting class sizes in the Foundation Stage, supporting a knowledge-based curriculum, and keeping SATs for pupils at the end of Key Stage 2.
- Incentivise teacher retention and recruitment, as well as improve the knowledge and skills of teachers, through the introduction of a bursary scheme to fund teachers to study for a higher degree and the introduction of in-service sabbaticals with a focus on professional development.

There is much here that is entirely appropriate, but the focus on behaviour and discipline betrays classic school-centric thinking. It might just be that the nature of schools themselves, for some pupils, is the major cause of inappropriate behaviour. The issue then is not to focus on behaviour per se, but rather on ensuring pupil engagement through a relevant curriculum, personalised learning strategies, and the involvement of family and community.

The drift to school-centric thinking

In most developed societies, children will spend around 200 days a year in school and be required to attend school for between 11 and 13 years. In effect this means that most children spend only 16% of their childhood years in school. Yet it is the school that government and society overwhelmingly focus on when we think about how learning takes place.

Children go to school to learn – of course. But this does not mean that they are not learning when they are not in school – quite the reverse. Children are always learning, and the 84% of their time that they are not in school (including time spent asleep) accounts for much of the learning that informs their ability to survive, develop and be successful as adults.

However, one of the characteristics of developed societies has been to move learning away from family and community, and so bureaucratise the components of the learning process. Indeed, one way to understand the most challenging interpretations of what it is like to experience school is to think about the extent to which school is formalised, bureaucratised and institutionalised.

Consider, for example, this list of features of the school-focused model of education:

- Prescribed ages to start and finish attending school, and specification of days and times for attendance.
- Automatic chronological cohort progression, focusing on the age of the group rather than the stage of development of individuals.
- A curriculum that advantages middle-class pupils, notably in terms of language development and life experiences.
- A reductionist definition of the curriculum.
- Control of the delivery and assessment of the curriculum.
- Generic provision that is non-negotiable based on an assumption of homogeneity rather than the reality of heterogeneity.
- Focus on employability and socialisation rather than personal development.

In effect, the school has become the central focus of control, while the role of the family and community in supporting learning has become marginalised in terms of official recognition. Family and community remain, however, highly significant in terms of their unseen influence. It is time now to rethink the balance.

5. Disentangling the Three Spheres of Influence

There is a very clear and sharp disagreement outside (though less so inside) the academic community about the relationship between the variables that determine academic success. The debate pivots around the relative influence of the school and of factors that are external to the school, notably the effect of social and economic variables. Government policy in England and many other developed countries in recent years has tended to place heavy emphasis on the school by supporting strategies that can be broadly described as school improvement. Indeed, for many years, government policy has in effect denied the possible influence of social and economic factors – the classic example being the various Ofsted inspection frameworks which never acknowledged that school context might have a relevant influence on school performance.

It is important to recognise that some school-improvement strategies have worked to a significant degree. For example, the 89% of schools in England in 2017 rated by Ofsted as 'good' or 'outstanding' represented a very real measure of success (at least by a narrow and limited definition of success). Yet equally the inspection framework makes no reference to securing social equity, and there is absolutely no guarantee that a 'good' or 'outstanding' school is a socially just school. The 11% of schools that do not fall into either of those categories also represent a long tail of low attainment that is a very high proportion relative to other countries and, crucially, reveal some very significant distortions. The Education Policy Institute's annual report for 2019 (Hutchinson et al. 2019, p.18) notes that in England:

- For the first time since 2011, progress in closing the GCSE attainment gap between disadvantaged pupils and their peers has come to a standstill. Between 2017 and 2018, the gap widened slightly by 0.2 months (to a gap of 18.1 months).
- There are large geographic variations, with a gap of over two years in some parts of the country and just six months in other areas.
- The gap in the early years has also stalled, widening slightly by 0.1 months to 4.5 months.
- Disadvantage gaps are larger, and are growing, in parts of the North.
- Black Caribbean pupils have experienced particularly poor progress, falling further behind white British pupils.
- Pupils with special educational needs remain the furthest behind.
- The most persistently disadvantaged pupils are almost two years (22.6 months) behind at the end of their GCSEs, and that gap has increased since 2011.

For a long time, the balance of influence between social factors and the school was generally seen as 80:20 (e.g. Silins and Mulford 2002, p.561), or in some cases 70:30 (e.g. Muijs 2010, p.89). However, recently Asbury and Plomin (2014; see also Plomin 2018) have introduced the need to start with the individual learner because of the impact of our genetic inheritance on educational outcomes. There is now increasing confidence that we can make even stronger assertions about the centrality and distinctiveness of the individual learner.[3]

For example, in a sample of 11,117 16-year-old twins drawn from the Twins Early Development Study, Plomin and Asbury found that heritability had a substantial influence on GCSE performance for core subjects (58%) as well as for each subject individually: English (52%), mathematics (55%) and science (58%). In contrast, the overall influence of a shared environment, which includes all family and school influences

3. 'Individual differences in educational achievement at the end of compulsory education are not primarily an index of the quality of teachers or schools: much more of the variance can be attributed to genetics than to school or family environment.' (Asbury and Plomin 2014, p.9)

shared by members of twin pairs growing up in the same family and attending the same school, accounts for about 36% of the variance of mean GCSE scores.

Figure 4 shows the relationship between the three spheres of influence affecting educational achievement: the influence of personal genetic factors, the influence of social and economic factors, and the influence of the school. There can be no precise or definitive statement about the relative weighting of each component – the diagram depicts putative rather than definitive ratios in an abstract environment.

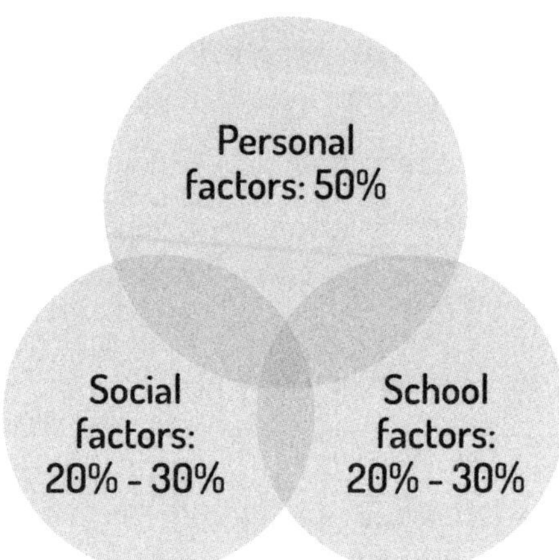

Figure 4: The Balance of Variables Influencing Academic Success

The relative weightings in Figure 4 point to the fact that, as the Audit Commission (2006) stressed, improvement cannot be achieved by schools acting alone, and the most significant factors may be beyond their current remit, capacity or commitment.

The core proposition for this chapter is that successful learning, of any type or subject, is the result of the complex interaction of these three variables: the school, the social and economic circumstances of the learners, and the individual learner herself or himself. Some schools (such as selective maintained schools or those in the independent sector) are able to create the optimum environmental circumstances through their ability to control their intake by ability or by positive social factors.

Others, perhaps the majority, are less fortunate.

It is the dynamic chemistry of these three spheres of influence that defines the work of the teacher and school leader. It is the need to exert a positive influence on the factors in each sphere that provides the key issue for school leadership and governance going forward. When the factors influencing a school's potential are largely positive, then the potential of that school to succeed academically are significantly enhanced. The negative corollary is equally true. Some factors are disproportionately significant. Overall, however, Desforges noted in his 2003 study that 'a great deal of the variation in students' achievement is outside of the school's influence' (Desforges and Abouchaar 2003, p.21).

Desforges' study drew the very robust conclusion that, in the primary years, the family is six times more significant than the school. Sadly, government policy was not able to come to terms with the potential challenge of such a finding, even though Sure Start and Every Child Matters, together with the concept of the extended school, showed the potential for a change of mindset.

In their blog *How much do schools matter?*, Wilkinson, Bryson and Stokes argue that:

> ... we do not identify any great increase in the importance of schools in explaining pupil attainment in England since 2003, despite an increased focus on school level interventions. Furthermore, the majority of pupil attainment is not accounted for by schools. Other studies point to other important factors such as genetics and family and neighbourhood ... as important predictors of pupil attainment. (Wilkinson et al. 2018)

To understand this more deeply, we will now look in turn at the significance of each of the three spheres of influence which contribute to educational success.

6. It's Personal: The First Sphere of Influence

In many ways, the provision of any service can be seen as a tension between the personal and the generic. The extent to which the prevailing culture of schooling is focused on the idiosyncratic needs of every pupil is a key factor in the extent to which it is possible to respond appropriately to the needs of the individual in a way that recognises and respects their uniqueness.

In his discussion of the complexities of modern medicine, Atul Gawande outlines the range of patients and their needs that he has had in his case load:

> In one day, I'd had six completely different primary medical problems and a total of 26 different additional diagnoses – it's tempting to believe that no one else's job could be as complex as mine. But extreme complexity is the rule for almost everyone. (Gawande 2011, p.21)

Gawande goes on to discuss the work of doctors in one American hospital that included seeing patients with an average range of 250 primary illnesses with 900 other active medical problems, for which they prescribed 300 medications and 100 different types of laboratory test. He also describes a study of 41,000 trauma patients that had '1224 different injury-related diagnoses in 32,261 unique combinations' (Gawande 2011, p.35). Effective medical care in A&E departments is based to a very significant extent on the rapidity and accuracy of diagnosis with appropriately prioritised interventions. Each patient's chance of recovery is directly related to the extent in which they are recognised and treated as a unique case.

This perspective is reinforced by a strategy developed in a number of hospital trusts working with older patients who have had hip-replacement surgery. There is an 11% mortality rate for such patients; about 4000 die each year within a month of surgery. The intervention that has reduced the mortality rate to 5.5% is based on a very simple premise: a fourth meal every day (Bodkin 2019). However, this extra meal is:

- sourced by a nutritional adviser
- negotiated with the patient based on their personal like and dislikes
- eaten in the presence of the adviser.

The impact of the strategy is shown in the reduction of the mortality rate and the reduction in the length of hospital stay from 25 to 20 days. It works largely because the patient is treated as an individual who is given the opportunity to make meaningful choices that have a genuine impact on their sense of wellbeing.

Every teacher and every parent is aware of just how different children can be. Even within a nuclear family there can be radical differences in all sorts of ways. And if even families are not homogeneous then there seems to be little chance of finding a homogeneous class in a school. It has long been recognised that effective teaching takes the differences in a class into account. The highly effective teacher knows her class and differentiates accordingly. High-quality teaching goes beyond the generic experience and creates a range of opportunities that respond to the needs of the individual. However, time, space and finite resources limit the possibility of responding to the uniqueness of every learner, unless there is a radical rethink as to how learning is organised.

The movement towards more evidence-informed practice in education has led to growing interest in the complex boundary between educational practice and increasingly robust scientific research. On average, in terms of their DNA sequence, all humans are 99.5% similar to any other human. Yet no two humans are genetically identical. For Asbury and Plomin, this has significant implications for our approach to schooling:

> The significance of our findings is that individual differences in educational achievement at the end of compulsory education are not primarily an index of the quality of teachers or schools: much more of the variance of GCSE scores can be attributed to genetics than to school or family environment. (Asbury and Plomin 2014, pp.11–12)

They continue:

> Our evidence makes it crystal clear that treating children as blank slates or empty vessels, using a factory model of schooling, and arbitrarily imposing the same targets for everyone, are approaches that work against, rather than with natural child development. Our schools and our educational policies will be improved if they are designed to respond to naturally occurring individual differences in ability and development.

This is, of course, a highly contested area with a great deal of work still to be done before the 'pure' research might be integrated into the mental models of teachers and directly inform their daily practice. The two key areas seem to be the significance of our genetic inheritance for learning and teaching and, similarly, the implications of cognitive neuroscience for our understanding of the nature of the learner:

> Individual differences are lost in stereotypes … there's no such thing as an average adolescent, and brain development varies widely between people. Research is starting to investigate what gives rise to these large individual differences – the person's genes, their specific environment – and the consequences of the individual brain's developmental trajectory across adolescence. (Blakemore 2019, p.202)

There are numerous variables that inform and influence our unique identity as learners. What makes the issue even more complex are the potential permutations emerging from the interaction of these variables. It is simply not practically possible (or morally acceptable) to subsume (in some sort of social blender) all the individual learner profiles in a class in a school to create an artificial sense of homogeneity. Asbury and Plomin suggest the need for a model of education that recognises the important role of genetics:

> Rather than a passive model of schooling as instruction (instruere, 'to build in'), we propose an active model of education (educare, 'to bring out') in which children create their own educational experiences in part on the basis of their genetic propensities, which supports the trend towards personalised learning. (Asbury and Plomin 2014, p.158)

We will return to that last sentence and its implications for educational practice in chapter 14. The issue here lies in identifying the relative significance of inherited and environmental factors. This is essentially the nature and nurture debate brought up to date. It is not a matter of either/or, but rather of nature *via* nurture. Nor, given the complexity of the human genome, is it a matter of arguing for personal interventions based purely on genetic data. In any case, while genes may be an important and under-recognised factor in educational achievement, they are not the only factor for us to consider.

7. Social Class, Poverty and the Second Sphere of Influence

The social context and circumstances into which we are born provide a second sphere of influence on educational achievement. To examine this proposition, we will consider here the impacts of social class and poverty.

Social class

The role and significance of social class in British society remains debateable and contested. For some it is a historical irrelevance, while for others it is a real expression of the factors that influence their daily lives and future prospects. However, if all the available evidence is taken into account, then the key insight is that provided by Wilkinson and Pickett (2010): 'more equal societies almost always do better'.

More so than in almost any other European country, inherited power, influence and wealth remain fundamental to how British society works (Verkaik 2018). According to the Sutton Trust and Social Mobility Commission's report *Elitist Britain*:

> The United Kingdom in 2019 is an increasingly divided nation. 2016's vote to leave the European Union both reflected and accentuated deep social divisions across the country. Britain's 'elite' is higher in the national consciousness than ever, with strained trust between significant sections of the population and those at the highest levels of politics, business and the media. Social mobility across the UK is low and not improving, depriving large parts of the country of

> opportunity, and contributing to this sense of distance. (The Sutton Trust and the Social Mobility Commission 2019, p.4)

The dominant conceptualisation of British society by the British themselves, as well as by outsiders, is of an essentially hierarchical and deferential society. Yet it must also be recognised that the historic tripartite division into working, middle and upper class is not an adequate framework to describe contemporary British society. For Wilkinson and Pickett:

> ... the UK is a rich country, but with many poor people. It's a largely happy country, but one with many unhappy people. Some inequalities and divergences of experience are inevitable. But they are much wider in the UK than they need to be, and the result is a great deal of unnecessary harm and suffering. (Wilkinson and Pickett 2009, p.84).

One of the intriguing, if not actually mystifying, aspects of British attitudes towards poverty is that it is not only inevitable but also the fault of the poor. Those who live in poverty are seen as in in some way bankrupt, morally as well as financially. While the spectre of the workhouse is a receding memory (the last workhouse closed in 1930), the negative connotations remain. At the other end of the scale are those enjoying positions of great power, wealth and social status. Verkaik (2018, p.4) observes that only 7% of the population attend a private school, yet private-school pupils represent 74% of senior judges, 71% of senior officers in the armed forces, 67% of Oscar winners, 55% of permanent secretaries, 50% of cabinet ministers and members of the House of Lords, and a third of Russell Group university vice-chancellors.

Britain is a society deeply rooted in inequality, and one in which wellbeing, for many, is elusive. One piece of academic research has been particularly significant in understanding the impact of social inequality. Originally carried out by Leon Feinstein, it analysed the results of the 1970 British Cohort Study, which tracked the development of British children at 22 months, 42 months, 5 years and 10 years.

Feinstein's conclusions were clear and unequivocal. The children of educated or wealthy parents who scored poorly in the early tests had a tendency to catch up, whereas the low-achieving children of worse-off parents were unlikely to do so. Early high-achievers from disadvantaged backgrounds were gradually overtaken by early low-achievers from advantaged families.

> On the most basic level such a system gravely offends the principles of equality of opportunity, the foundation of any democracy. It is also a form of corruption because it permits people to bypass the rules of professional advancement by paying membership fees to a self-selecting group of lottery winners. (Verkaik 2018, p.309)

Hart and Risley (2003) established from the longitudinal data that the problem of skill differences among children at the time of school entry is bigger, more intractable and more important than had previously been thought. So much is happening to children during their first three years at home, at a time when they are especially malleable and uniquely dependent on the family for virtually all their experience, that by the age of three, an intervention must address not just a lack of knowledge or skill, but also an entire general approach to experience.

What is very clear from this data is that parenting is significantly influenced by social norms and behaviour patterns. This explains the varying degrees of engagement with children in terms of language development. For example, 86% to 98% of the words recorded in a child's vocabulary are also recorded in the parent's vocabulary. This reinforces the importance of the literacy of the home. The vocabulary of the child of professional parents at 1116 words compares with the child whose parents are on welfare at 525 words. That gap does much to explain why social class can have a life-long impact – it takes a very long time to compensate for such a start. Even more worrying is the ratio of affirmations and prohibitions that a four-year-old child is exposed to – a ratio of 32 affirmations to 5 prohibitions for the child with professional parents, and a ratio of 5 affirmations to 11 prohibitions for the child of parents on benefits. A rich vocabulary and saturation in language, combined with positive experiences of communication, might explain much of the success of the middle classes.

Another variable that serves to reinforce and illuminate class differences is the number of books in a household. Sikora (2018) found a high correlation between the number of books in a household and levels of literacy, numeracy and ICT skills. Teenagers with lower levels of secondary education, but who grew up in a home filled with books, became as literate, numerate and technologically apt in adulthood as university graduates who grew up with only a few books. The broad conclusion of the research is that a 'bookish' adolescence makes for a good deal of educational advantage.[4] Clearly, books do not only furnish a room; they are also a significant variable in enhancing academic performance – yet another factor beyond the scope of the school.

The BBC LAB UK's Great British Class Survey offers an updated and more empirically based survey of current British society (Savage et al. 2013). The critical point is that the elite persists as it does in few other modern democratic societies. Although the labels might change, the overall balance of British society remains in the favour of the elite and established middle class:

- **Elite:** the most privileged group in the UK, distinct from the other six classes through its wealth. This group has the highest levels of economic, social and cultural capital and comprises roughly 6% of the total population.
- **Established middle class:** the second wealthiest group, scoring highly on all three capitals. Also the largest and most gregarious group, scoring second highest for cultural capital (25% of the population).
- **Technical middle class:** a small, distinctive, new class group which is prosperous but scores low for social and cultural capital. Distinguished by its social isolation and cultural apathy (6% of the population).
- **New affluent workers:** a young class group which is socially and culturally active, with middling levels of economic capital (15% of the population).

4. '... respondents' education, occupational status and reading activities at home are strong predictors of superior literacy nearly everywhere, but respondents clearly benefit from adolescent exposure to books above and beyond these effects.' (Sikora 2018, p.4)

- **Traditional working class:** scores low on all forms of capital but is not completely deprived. Its members have reasonably high house values, explained by this group having the oldest average age at 66 (14% of the population).
- **Emergent service workers:** a new, young, urban class group which is relatively poor but has high social and cultural capital (19% of the population).
- **Precariat, or precarious proletariat:** the poorest, most deprived class group, scoring low for social and cultural capital (15% of the population).

For most of these classes, education is a positive and significant element of their identity and value system. The precariat (a portmanteau word combining 'precarious' with 'proletariat') are generally seen as victims of neo-liberal approaches to society and economics. Members of the precariat are, literally, on the bottom rung of every ladder and have the lowest levels of economic, social and cultural capital. The precariat have a view of education that is the antithesis of that of the other classes (especially the elite and established middle class). Being a member of the precariat:

> ... intensifies a sense of alienation and instrumentality in what they have to do. There is no 'shadow of the future' hanging over their actions, to give them a sense that what they say or do or feel today will have a binding effect on their longer-term relationships. (Standing 2011, p.12)

Standing goes on to describe how the precariat experiences 'the four A's – anger, anomie, anxiety and alienation' (Standing 2011, p.19). It is not difficult to find the practical expression of these A's in the impact on the children of the precariat and their attitudes towards school.

Poverty

The Joseph Rowntree Foundation's annual report UK Poverty 2018 is quite explicit about the level of child poverty in the UK:

> In our society, child poverty has been rising since 2011/12. 4.1 million children now live in poverty, a rise of 500,000 in the last five years. The vast majority of this rise has taken place in working families. (Joseph Rowntree Foundation 2018, p.49)

In effect, this means that about one third of children live in poverty (9 out of every class of 30). Nearly half of children in single-parent families in the UK live in poverty, compared with one in four children in couple families. Over the last five years, poverty rates for children in single-parent families have risen by around twice as much as those for children in couple families.

There are several defining characteristics about the attitude to child poverty in the UK. The first issue is the extent to which child poverty is tolerated, indeed accepted and embedded, as the basis for how British society works. From this perspective, child poverty is inevitable and inescapable. Secondly, since the Tudor poor laws, poverty in the UK has been seen as primarily a moral issue; that is, poverty is the blameworthy result of a feckless and indolent underclass. Thirdly, there is a belief in a taxation system that enables the rich to become richer in the erroneous belief that everyone benefits. In fact, the gap between richest and poorest widens and creates a deeply systemic polarisation.[5]

Recent research carried out by the Chartered Institute of Personnel and Development (2019) discovered that the ratio of median FTSE 100 CEO pay to median UK full-time or part-time worker pay, although reduced from 167:1 in 2016, was still 117 times bigger in 2019. In practical terms, this means that the lowest-paid worker will have to work for 117 years to earn the same as the highest paid in one year. This polarity is reflected in many different measures, notably gender and geography (the North–South divide).

From an education perspective, the gap between North and South that characterised England in the nineteenth century remains as deep as ever.

5. 'But there remains a six-fold difference between the incomes of the top 20% of households and those of the bottom 20% … Inequalities of wealth, meanwhile, are even larger than those of income. 44% of the UK's wealth is owned by just 10% of the population, five times the total wealth held by the poorest half.' (IPPR Commission on Economic Justice 2018, pp.17–18)

This gap can only be understood in social and economic terms; it is not cultural but rather reflects the economic and social balance of England and of the North of England – there are significant regional variations in the North that reflect the contextual factors. The disparity between the North and South of England has long been understood; in 2016, Sir Michael Wilshaw, commenting on his final annual report as Her Majesty's Chief Inspector of Schools, said:

> In my last year's annual report, I said that there was a growing geographical divide in educational standards, after the age of 11, between the North, the Midlands and the South of England. We are fast becoming a tale of two countries in relation to our secondary school performance compounded by woeful vocational provision at both pre-16 and post-16 levels. (Wilshaw 2016).

It is therefore perhaps reasonable to argue that school improvement as a pervasive strategy works only in areas that are socially propitious, and the majority of these areas are in the South of England. Certainly, school improvement seems to have been less successful when looking at the education of children growing up in poverty.[6]

The obvious implications of living in poverty might include some or all of the following:

- Financial insecurity; no consistency or predictability of income.
- Vulnerability to loan sharks and high-interest loans.
- Being disadvantaged by benefits bureaucracy, e.g. delayed benefit payments.
- Problems with budgeting and making the money last the week.
- Not having the money to buy healthy food and so struggling to prepare nutritious and economical meals.
- Financial crises, e.g. white goods breaking down, shoes wearing out.
- Poor-quality accommodation and high rents.

6. 'Poor children still have worse educational outcomes at every stage and we have a long tail of low attainment – 17% of UK students fail to reach 'modern functional literacy', compared to just 11% in Canada.' (DfE 2016, p.6)

- No holidays.
- No savings or capacity to plan for an alternative future.

Underpinning all of these factors is long-term stress, tension and anxiety, and a loss of personal confidence and personal efficacy. In some respects, this leads to victimhood and compromised personal agency. The specific issues at school for children living in poverty might include:

- Having poor physical health.
- Experiencing mental-health problems.
- Having a low sense of wellbeing.
- Underachieving in their work.
- Experiencing social deprivation.
- Feeling unsafe.
- Suffering stigma and bullying at school (The Children's Society 2019).

The net cumulative result can be to create a self-reinforcing, vicious spiral of negativity that compounds all of the other factors we have been discussing. Poverty has a multiplier effect in that it negatively reinforces the potentially problematic influence of economic uncertainty and vulnerability.

A further example of how poverty exacerbates the gap in terms of social equity is the phenomenon of additional funding for maintained schools, largely through parent-teacher associations (PTAs). According to the *Guardian* (Ferguson and McIntyre 2019), England's 30 most successful PTAs raised £3.6m in a single year. These schools are predominantly in the South East of England, with none in the North. The majority of the schools were rated 'outstanding' by Ofsted with the rest all being 'good'. Across these schools, only 5% of their pupils qualified for the pupil premium. One school raised £894,000 and another £631,770. This, of course, does not take into consideration the extra funding through endowments and legacies that is such an important feature of independent schools. In essence, in a low-equity society like Britain, wealth secures and sustains a disproportionate advantage.

Ivan Illich perhaps offers us the last word, though regrettably many years have since passed he wrote it:

> It should be obvious that, even with schools of equal quality, a poor child can seldom catch up with a rich one. Even if they attend equal schools and begin at the same age, poor children lack most of the educational opportunities which are casually available to the middle-class child. (Illich 1970, p.12)

According to one 2013 calculation in the United States (ExpandED Schools 2013), that difference in educational opportunity for a middle-class child equates to an extra 6000 learning hours by age 11.

8. Family Matters Too

The youngest children have a powerful evolutionary imperative to learn; learning is what they do all day, every day. However, their context can have an enormous impact on the quality of that learning. Just as wise and prudent people know that prevention is better than cure and so have their cars serviced or receive their annual flu jab, so wise societies invest in the earliest forms of educational provision. This is not so much because prevention is better than cure as because 'predict and prevent' is better than 'find and fix'.

The key rationale for early-years provision is that it stops things going wrong rather than having to put things right. This is the same philosophy that underpins airline safety, food preparation, and the design and building of any form of domestic appliance. Preventing failure is morally, economically and socially preferable to having to put things right later.

Appropriate provision in the early years can therefore be seen as a moral imperative as much as an economic or social imperative. The success and effectiveness of societies and communities is significantly influenced and informed by the extent to which early-years education is accorded appropriate status and resource.[7]

There is a direct and explicit correlation between inequalities in the early years and inequalities in later life. Investment in early-years education is

---

7. 'The early years are not only critical for life chances: inequalities at this age perpetuate throughout life. Improving experiences in the early years is central to reducing inequalities in childhood and later life. Children from the lowest income households have an average percentile score on school readiness that is more than 30 points below their peers in the first quartile, and their vocabulary at age three is more than 20 points below their peers.' (Bowers and Strelitz 2012, p.8)

not only a critical element in securing a more equitable society, it is also a potent way of reducing the costs of failure in society.

Although it is not inevitable or predestined, there is a very clear causal relationship between early disadvantage and subsequent systemic failure. The rate of learning and development in the early years is greater than at any other time in a person's life. It is during this period that children experience potentially rapid cognitive, linguistic, social, emotional and motor development that cannot be replicated in later years. Although some amelioration of disadvantage is possible in later life, it can never fully compensate. This period in a child's development involves the emergence of increasingly rich language skills, complex social behaviours, emotional capacities, problem-solving abilities and pre-literacy skills.

There is an overwhelming consensus that investment in learning in the pre-school years is one of the most powerful strategies available to a society to maximise life chances and wellbeing, and educational and economic success, as well as to reduce social dysfunctionality.[8] For Graham Allen, this is a primary justification for an integrated strategy of intervention in order to minimise the potentially negative impact of social and economic circumstances:

> The rationale is simple: many of the costly and damaging social problems in society are created because we are not giving children the right type of support in their earliest years, when they should achieve their most rapid development. If we do not provide that help early enough, then it is often too late. (Allen 2011, p.xiii)

Allen goes on to provide specific examples from research that help to demonstrate the potentially substantial negative implications of failing to engage:

- A child's development score at just 22 months can serve as an accurate predictor of educational outcomes at 26 years.

8. 'The chances of starting school ready to learn are worse for children from the poorest households. A child's brain undergoes its most rapid growth in the years before they start school and research has shown that children living in poverty often start school academically behind their better-off peers. The gap in achievement can be seen from as early as 22 months.' (Minogue and Moore 2013, p.1)

- Babies are born with 25% of their brains developed, and there is then a rapid period of development so that by the age of three their brains are 80% developed.
- During that period, neglect, the wrong type of parenting, and other adverse experiences can have a profound effect on how children are emotionally 'wired'. This will deeply influence their future responses to events and their ability to empathise with other people.
- Early intervention to promote social and emotional development can significantly improve mental and physical health, educational attainment and employment opportunities. Early intervention can also help to prevent criminal behaviour (especially violent behaviour), drug and alcohol misuse and teenage pregnancy.

There is now abundant evidence to show that development of children depends highly on the engagement of their mothers.[9] Although effective parenting is fundamental to cognitive and social development, it would be very wrong to assume that such parenting is widely available across society.[10] A crucial role of early-years provision is therefore not just to make high-quality education available, but also to provide support to families and communities to contribute to the development of children in every context of their lives.

According to the Effective Pre-school, Primary and Secondary Education project at the Institute of Education, London, which has tracked more than 3000 children since 1997:

> There is an enduring effect of pre-school education. Attendance, quality and duration at pre-school all show long-term effects on students' academic outcomes. (Institute for Effective Education, 2014)

---

9. 'Families play a role in this process that is far more important than the role of schools. There are multiple skills and multiple abilities that are important for adult success … Skill attainment at one stage of the life cycle raises skill attainment at later stages of the life cycle (self-productivity).' (Cunha et al. 2005, p.1)

10. 'Today's rising generation is the first in which a majority are spending a large part of early childhood in some form of out-of-home childcare. At the same time, neuroscience research is demonstrating that loving, stable, secure, and stimulating relationships with caregivers in the earliest months and years of life are critical for every aspect of a child's development.' (Adamson 2008, p.3)

The boost from pre-school education is equivalent to gaining seven B grades at GCSE rather than seven C grades. Children who go to pre-school also develop better literacy, behaviour and concentration as teenagers, and can earn an extra £27,000 over their working lives, the research found. What is clear is that it is not just the rather narrow (though still significant) outcomes in terms of GCSE performance, but rather the potential impact on children's life chances and wellbeing, that validate early-years provision.

In terms of cognitive development, experiences are sequential and cumulative. Experiences in infancy establish habits of seeking, noticing and incorporating new and more complex experiences, as well as schemas for categorising and thinking about experiences. Neurologically, infancy is a critical period because cortical development is influenced by the amount of central nervous system activity stimulated by experience. Therefore, effective parenting for literacy and oracy would seem to involve such activities as:

- Making eye contact as early as possible and holding sustained conversations using words and sounds.
- Having play 'books' available from the earliest stages of development.
- Making stories an essential element of domestic routines.
- Reading together.
- Singing and giving non-stop commentaries on car journeys.

On the basis of this review of the broad issues informing the debate about early-years care and provision, it is possible to make a number of assertions about the nature of high-quality early-years provision:

- All provision starts from the premise of recognising every child as a unique individual, to be treated with appropriate dignity.

- Learning in the early years is the result of the interaction of a complex range of variables that all need to be positive to secure optimum outcomes.
- Parents have to be seen as co-educators or partners in learning. The wellbeing of mothers is an essential component of success in early-years provision.
- Effective learning cannot be divorced from social, physical and psychological wellbeing.
- For learning to have a long-term influence, it has to be rooted in social interaction through play and language development.
- Early-years learning has to be seen as valid in its own right and not just as the preparation for the next stage of schooling.
- The outcomes of early-years education have to be judged on the basis of qualitative and formative approaches rather than quantitative and summative judgments.

In order to achieve these educationally and socially aspirational outcomes, traditional modes of provision may not be adequate; indeed, historical patterns of provision may actually have real contraindications. Many of the perceived issues with early-years provision can often be related to the failure to see the child as a unique individual and to design services around the child rather than around professional structures and models of provision.

Family is of almost primal significance in terms of the potential for effective learning to take place and, equally, for schooling to work to optimum effect. In fact, Desforges and Abouchaar (2003) argue on the basis of rigorous empirical and statistically robust data that the family is six times more significant than the school.[11] They highlight that the key element in school improvement and any movement towards securing equity and excellence is a focus on family and community issues.

11. 'In the primary age range the impact caused by different levels of parental involvement is much bigger than differences associated with variations in the quality of schools.' (Desforges and Abouchaar 2003, p.21)

In their study of unequal and polarised societies, Wilkinson and Pickett come to exactly the same conclusion as Desforges and Abouchaar:

> Although good schools make a difference, the biggest influence on educational attainment, how well a child performs in school and later in higher education, is family background. (Wilkinson and Pickett 2010, p.103)

9. The Impact on Schools: The Third Sphere of Influence

We can now begin to better understand the impact of all these factors in the first two spheres of influence on schools, which provide the third and, in relative terms, probably least significant sphere of influence in terms of educational achievement.

The use of the provision of free school meals as a measure of poverty is unsatisfactory in a number of respects, but it does at least provide a broad comparative measure. This measure, often referred to as the 'gap', provides a very clear indication of the relative performance of children from poor families (although the claimed number of such children cannot be regarded as definitive).

The evidence clearly shows that not only has the achievement gap not closed over the past ten years in England, neither has the social gap. Indeed, the level of child poverty actually grew in this period, potentially exacerbating the gap in terms of educational achievement. Children on free school meals continue to underachieve, regardless of whether the school they attend is rated highly by Ofsted or not.

Steve Strand (2016) argues the stubbornness of the attainment gap across all types of schools suggests that the quality of a school is not enough to overcome a disadvantaged background. His paper challenges the current narrative, favoured by politicians of all parties, that schools are 'failing' when they do not close the gap between disadvantaged pupils and their wealthier peers in terms of academic outcomes. Instead, he suggests, factors outside the school, rather than anything happening in the classroom, may be the root cause of attainment gaps.

Strand's analysis shows that the performance gap between pupils eligible for free school meals and those who are not is remarkably consistent, no matter how the school is rated by Ofsted. 'Good' and 'outstanding' schools may raise the bar for pupils, but they do not close the gap. Schools that are categorised as 'requires improvement' have a gap in terms of GCSE performance of 22% for pupil-premium students compared with a high of 56% for non-pupil-premium students. 'Outstanding' schools, however, have an average level of performance of 77% for non-pupil-premium students, but a gap of 27% in the relative performance of pupil-premium-students, leading Strand to the conclusion that:

> ... while the most effective schools may raise the achievement of disadvantaged pupils, non-disadvantaged pupils may benefit just as much, so that these school do not eliminate the achievement gap. In short, the relative performance of the disadvantaged remains similar even when the absolute performance of such groups has improved ... [This may] indicate that there are substantial influences beyond the school gates which are outside the control of schools. (Strand 2016, p.140)

It therefore seems reasonable to argue that the gap will not be closed, nor will the tail of underachievement be shortened, by focusing on school improvement alone. It is of course vital to ensure that schools are operating to optimal effectiveness, working to secure equity and to secure the best possible life chances for every pupil. But, in order to achieve further real improvement, it is necessary to focus on factors other than the school; notably the social and economic circumstances of pupils and their engagement with (and disposition towards) learning. The Audit Commission's 2006 report *More Than the Sum* reinforces this perspective:

> Traditional school improvement activity has tended to concentrate on teaching and learning at individual school level. Critical though this is, by itself the approach is limited ... Children's educational underachievement is linked with a wide range of deprivation factors: low parental qualifications, poor housing conditions, low family income, ill-health, family problems and wider community factors such as low aspirations and unemployment. (Audit Commission 2006, p.2)

The report concluded that school improvement and renewal are inseparable issues from neighbourhood improvement and renewal, particularly in the most disadvantaged areas.

This is not an argument for saying that what happens in school has no influence at all. Of course there is a very clear need to ensure that the potential 20–30% that a school can influence is working to optimum effect; that the school works effectively to control and influence that which can be controlled and influenced. There is increasing confidence in identifying those aspects of leadership and management within the school that are most likely to optimise the overall academic performance of the school and of disadvantaged and vulnerable children in particular.

Research undertaken by the National Foundation for Educational Research identified seven factors that are common in schools which are more successful in raising disadvantaged pupils' attainment (DfE 2015):

1. **A whole-school ethos of attainment for all.** More successful schools have an ethos of high attainment for all pupils. They view each pupil as an individual and consciously avoid stereotyping disadvantaged pupils by referring to them as a group.
2. **Addressing behaviour and attendance.** Pupils have to be in school and able to pay attention before they can access learning. More successful schools make sure they have really effective behaviour strategies, such as communicating simple, clear rules and training all staff in behaviour management.
3. **High-quality teaching for all.** Leaders of more successful schools emphasise the importance of 'quality teaching first'. They aim to provide a consistently high standard through setting expectations, monitoring performance, tailoring teaching and support to suit their pupils, and sharing best practice.
4. **Meeting individual learning needs.** More successful schools see pupils as individuals, each with their own challenges, talents and interests. Staff work to identify what might help each pupil to make the next steps in their learning, whether they are performing below, at or above expectations. Staff focus on providing targeted support for under-performing pupils during curriculum time.

5. **Deploying staff effectively.** More successful schools identify the strengths of each member of staff and find the best ways to use them. Such schools are quick to spot potential and to 'grow their own staff'. They devolve as much responsibility as possible to frontline staff and deploy their best teachers to work with pupils who need the most support.
6. **Data driven and responding to evidence.** More successful schools use data to identify pupils' learning needs at every opportunity – when pupils join the school, during regular reviews of progress and during day-to-day teaching.
7. **Clear, responsive leadership.** Senior leaders in more successful schools ensure that staff are willing to do whatever it takes to help each pupil to succeed. They hold every staff member accountable for pupils' progress.

We draw on elements of all of these throughout the course of this book in our analysis of the next steps to take. However, as Part Two has repeatedly shown, on its own this by itself will not be enough to take us to the next stage, in just the same way as travel times in years gone by were not improved by producing faster horses. That improvement came from developing something fundamentally different: the internal combustion engine, with its hugely greater horsepower.

Our task in education now is to find and deploy such a key to change.

10. Social Capital and the Key to Change

It is time to home in on the essence of the question posed to us by Charles Fadel in the Introduction. If what the theory and what the research are telling us is correct, then schools need to pay greater attention to their interaction with the other two spheres of influence if we are to get to the next level of school improvement. They must become builders of social capital.

By social capital we mean the potential capacity for people to engage most effectively with each other, through the development of high-quality relationships based on trust, shared norms and values, and open communication expressed through networks and interdependent relationships.

Therein lies the key we are seeking. The school which is able to build the right sort of social capital inside itself then becomes able to turn itself inside out, so as to contribute to building social capital around it. This in turn leads over time to the next stage of school improvement.

Community matters more than we often think:

> The community … plays a number of important roles in society. It anchors the individual in real human networks and gives them a sense of identity; our presence in the world is verified by our impact on people around us … our community gives us a sense of self-determination, a sense of direct control over our lives. (Rajan 2019, p.xv)

Rajan goes on to point out that, even in the best resourced localities, community 'fills the gaps' in terms of care and support. George Monbiot (2018) reports a study in Frome in Somerset which suggests that where isolated people who have health problems are supported by community groups and volunteers, the number of emergency admissions to hospital falls 'spectacularly'. Across the whole of Somerset during the period of the study such admissions rose by 29%, but in Frome they fell by 17%. Living in a community with high social capital is literally good for you.

Rishi Manchanda (2014) demonstrates that many medical ills are significantly pre-empted or cured by social rather than medical interventions. In other words, bad housing, poverty and a dysfunctional community have negative psychological and physical manifestations. Living in a community is not just a social benefit; it offers physical and psychological benefits as well. Of course, this has been known since the very earliest emergence of Homo sapiens, when an obvious genetic advantage led to a predisposition to living in a community.

The potential benefits of community can be summarised as follows:

- Life expectancy is significantly enhanced.
- Mental health is likely to be good.
- People are less likely to fall ill and more likely to recover from serious illness.
- Employment will tend to be higher.
- Criminality and therefore victimhood will be lower.
- Children are more likely to be educationally successful.
- Cultural capital will be more readily available.
- Overall wellbeing will be higher.

Although problematic in terms of its evidential and conceptual foundations, Maslow's hierarchy (1943) does reinforce the importance of social relationships in personal wellbeing and effectiveness. Once the basic biological and physiological needs have been met – such as food, shelter and sleep – and a person's basic safety is guaranteed, then relationships assume a high status and significance. The need to belong becomes a driving force, involving friendship, intimacy, trust, acceptance, and the receiving and giving of affection and love.

Affiliation with a community and being part of a group become essential elements of selfhood and personal development. Children that grow up with a strong sense of their own value and significance within the context of a healthy and effective community can have a significantly enhanced social potential.

This perspective is reinforced by a study carried out in Michigan, USA (Goddard et al. 2009), which found that social capital has a three to five times larger effect than financial capital on reading and maths scores. The broad conclusion is that the quality of relationships is more significant than financial capital:

> Social capital was not only more important to learning than instructional expenditures but also more important than the schools' poverty, ethnic make-up, or prior achievement. (Goddard et al. 2009)

As a generic concept, 'capital' refers to the capacity and resources that are available to support any human activity, enterprise or relationship. In the past the term was most frequently employed in the fields of business and economics, but it is now widely defined in terms of social potential as much as economic behaviour. Bourdieu (1986) identified three types of capital: economic, social and cultural. Hargreaves and Fullan (2012) extend this list to include professional, human, social and decisional capital. They argue that professional capital is a product of the interaction of human, social and decisional capital.

As a general rule, the more capital the better, so a great deal of energy is devoted in society to the acquisition and growth of capital resources. Just as start-up businesses need financial capital, so stressed communities need the development of social capital, and ambitious but disadvantaged young people need to build personal cultural capital.

The essential characteristics of each form of capital are summarised in Table 1.

Economic capital	Access to financial resources, economic reserves and markets
Social capital	The integrity of relationships, trust and authentic communication
Cultural capital	Personal knowledge, skills and behaviours
Human capital	The availability of people with knowledge, skills and experience
Professional capital	Work-related knowledge and expertise
Decisional capital	The ability to understand complex situations and make appropriate, effective and valid decisions

Table 1: Six Forms of Capital

Obviously there are significant overlaps in the components of each type of capital, and the table does not represent the very high levels of interdependence that are characteristic to how societies and communities actually operate. But what is very clear, and fundamental to this discussion, is that there is a very robust correlation between any successful community or organisation and high levels of capital, notably social capital. A community is a community because it has high social capital. This is seen through the nature and quality of social interactions and the relative levels and integrity of relationships, networks and trust.

It is worth remembering, however, that capital in itself is essentially neutral. It is the application of values to that capital that distinguishes between the criminal gang and the democratic society. For example, one of the defining features of terrorist groups is very high social capital. They are 'successful' in the extent to which they secure total commitment. However, such commitment is based on coercion and the abuse of power. In the context of this discussion, power has to be understood in Berry's terms:

> Such a community has the power – not invariably, but as a rule – to enforce decency without litigation. It has the power, that is, to influence behaviour. And it exercises this power not by coercion or violence but by teaching the young, and by preserving stories and

songs that tell (among other things) what works and does not work in a given place. (Berry 1992, pp.119–120)

In other words, although any group exercises a degree of power over its members, in a community with high social capital, this is based on human values. One key way to understand what is often described as the 'human side of enterprise' lies in the description of social interaction in terms of 'bonding' or 'bridging'; in essence, the extent to which we are inclined to engage or disengage with each other (that is, to collaborate).

Bonding social capital defines the extent to which a community has internal integrity and coherence. Bridging social capital defines the extent to which a community is willing to engage with other communities. This difference in perspective might be best understood in terms of collaboration within boundaries or between horizons.

The bonding community is essentially introverted, and usually for a very good reason. People living in a bonding community tend to have a far better quality of life but, crucially, this is reinforced and extended if the community can both bond and bridge.

The bridging community is essentially extroverted. It is confident in working beyond its own boundaries and favours interdependence between communities as a preferred mode of functioning. Healthy and mature communities tend to be confident and secure in their own identity and so are able to engage with other communities. Table 2 summarises the key differences between bonding and bridging social capital.

Bonding (autonomy)	Bridging (interdependency)
• Inward looking/introverted	• Outward looking/extroverted
• Competitive	• Cooperative
• Potentially exclusive	• Inclusive
• Self-reinforcing and legitimating	• Pluralist and consensual
• Homogeneous	• Heterogeneous

Table 2: Bonding and Bridging Social Capital

A bridging community is likely to be more successful than a bonding one, as shown in the example of Easter Island. Jared Diamond, in his discussion of the factors that influenced the disastrous collapse of the astonishing civilisation of Easter Island, points to 'a focus on statue construction ... and competition between the clans and chiefs driving the erection of bigger statues' (Diamond 2005, p.119). Thus, the combination of bonding and competition led to the complete collapse of what had been a sophisticated and very successful civilisation.

A major theme which we will develop throughout the remainder of the book is that this distinction and interaction between bonding and bridging, between exclusivity and inclusivity, has real significance for schools today in terms of the way they work and the way they are organised. A self-assessment tool which you may wish to consider in the context of your school, and which draws together all of the facets wrapped up in this idea, can be found at the end of chapter 14.

The significance of trust

In many respects, trust is the sine qua non of any definition of social capital and a clear and definitive criterion for a successful community. Trust is one of the essential components of social capital, which in turn is fundamental to collaboration. We collaborate in order to create a community; the success of any community is contingent on the depth and integrity of that cooperation. The more successful we are at learning to cooperate, the more likely it is that we will achieve a depth of collaboration that supports the promise of living and working in a community.

Trust combines the potential for significant rewards with an equally high degree of subjectivity, ambiguity and fragility. It takes a great deal of time to develop and embed, and yet can be easily destroyed because of inappropriate language, misunderstanding or accident. As Fullan (2010) puts it, 'trust comes after good experiences'. One of the key characteristics of community leaders is their ability to secure, consolidate and celebrate those good experiences.

A high level of trust is the basis of loving relationships, doctor-patient relationships, and any form of social exchange or transaction. Our level of personal wellbeing is directly correlated with the level of trust in our lives, irrespective of our age or status. Living and working in an effective community, high in social capital, in one of the very best ways of securing optimum levels of trust and wellbeing.

In Figure 5, trust is viewed as the interaction of four key variables:

- Credibility: the extent to which colleagues have integrity and authenticity.
- Consistency: predictability, reliability.
- Competence: demonstrated professional ability and expertise.
- Capacity: resilience and sustainability to secure trust over time.

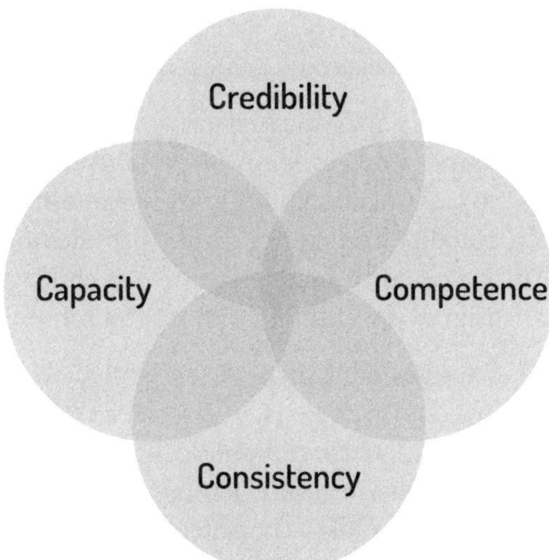

Figure 5: The Components of Trust and Their Interaction

The interaction between credibility, consistency, competence and capacity generates the confidence that in turn generates trust. A high level of trust results from the positive, mutual reinforcement of the four elements. This in turn generates further confidence in individuals and in the identity of the community, which in turn has positive effects on the performance of the community and individuals. It has created a virtuous spiral.

And this is directly true of schools, as Day and colleagues make clear in their study of the impact of leadership on pupil outcomes:

> Some recent studies show that trust remains a powerful and strong predictor of student achievement even after the effects of student background, prior achievement, race, and gender have been taken into account. Therefore, school leaders need to pay careful attention to the trust they engender in teachers, students, and parents if they wish to improve organisational performance still further. (Day et al. 2009, pp.244–245)

Shared values

There are two key questions around the development of shared values in the building of social capital: firstly, what those values should actually be, and secondly, how consensus is to be achieved and sustained.

For most purposes, values in education pivot around the concept of equity. Political discourse tends to focus on equality, but it is equity that is significant in terms of social capital and community building. The difference between equality and equity can be best demonstrated in the following proposition: equality means that every child goes to school, while equity means that every child goes to a good school.

The OECD (2015) describes education in the United Kingdom as being 'high performance, low equity'. This is, of course, a reflection of a British society which, in economic, social and political terms, is a long way from equity. In many ways, schools are just a microcosm of broader social trends. However, we believe schools do have the potential to become communities based in equity if they apply the principles discussed in this chapter.

For all practical purposes, contemporary liberal democracies focus on a range of virtues that seem to be deeply consensual, if not actually self-legitimating:

> A community identifies itself by an understood mutuality of interests. But it lives and acts by the common virtues of trust, goodwill, forbearance, self-restraint, compassion, and forgiveness. If it hopes to continue long as a community, it will wish to – and will have to – encourage respect

> for all its members, human and natural. It will encourage respect for all stations and occupations. (Berry 1992, pp.119–120)

One of the most significant and powerful variables in understanding the potential of social capital is the extent to which there is a significant degree of consensus and homogeneity around the core values which inform all dimensions of social interaction. In many respects, the highest levels of social capital, and so the most effective communities, are associated with shared beliefs and consensual morality. There are numerous historical and contemporary examples of highly successful communities that demonstrate moral hegemony and explicit cultural norms. Equally, there are examples of social groups that have failed because of the inability to secure agreement on core values.

An obvious success story in terms of educational performance in recent years has been Finland. There are many factors that explain Finland's consistently high performance, but one of the defining characteristics of Finnish society is a high degree of moral consensus:

> Finland is, however, very unique in terms of its values, cultural determinants and social cohesion ... Fairness, honesty and social justice are deeply rooted in the Finnish way of life. People have a strong sense of shared responsibility, not only for their own lives but for the lives of others. Fostering the wellbeing of children starts before they are born and continues until adulthood. (Sahlberg 2011, p.12)

Finnish society is highly homogeneous (although this is changing to some extent) and it is based on a high degree of consensus around core values. In any social context in Finland there appears to be a very high correlation between explicit values based on consensus and high performance.[12] In contrast, organisations that are heterogeneous and

12. 'The high quality and performance of Finland's educational system cannot be divorced from the clarity, characteristics of, and broad consensus about the country's broader social vision ... There is compelling clarity about and commitment to inclusive, equitable and innovative social values beyond as well as within the educational system.' (Pont et al. 2008, p.80) 'It is hard to imagine how Finland's educational success could be achieved or maintained without reference to the nation's broader system of distinctive social values that more individualistic and inequitable societies may find it difficult to accept.' (Pont et al. 2008, p.92)

unable to achieve consensus are rarely high performing as they spend much of the time debating, negotiating and contesting their core purpose and principles; in essence, storming rather than performing.

In terms of the values that are most appropriate in an educational context, there can never be complete agreement. Indeed, ongoing dialogue is essential to a vibrant community that seeks to improve itself. However, that dialogue is also important in reinforcing and consolidating shared values which serve as the basis for professional and leadership practice.

In a society that is as richly pluralistic and individualistic as Britain, securing any degree of moral hegemony is fundamentally challenging. The debates about the nature of education since 2010 bear witness to the fact that, unlike Finland, education in Britain (and particularly England) is deeply contentious and politically divisive. So the notion of a national moratorium on change in national educational policy in England is at best naïve, at worst Panglossian.

One potential source for some sort of consensus, which has not been given the respect it deserves, is the Cambridge Primary Review. Through evidence-informed analysis, rigorous review and sustained focus, the Review provides a major resource. In particular, it offers a set of principles that would seem to command almost universal respect. Although the Review focused on primary education, much of its work is directly applicable to all fields of education.

A much-abbreviated summary of the Review's proposals (Alexander 2010) (see Figure 6) indicates its potential as a starting point for conversations about community and school values. Taken together, values and aspirations such as these fill a crucial role in developing social capital and thus effective communities. They act as the 'social glue' that binds a community, and they also create the common language that is essential to developing social capital. One of the pivotal roles for community leaders is to build a shared vocabulary around core values that enhances the quality of dialogue. Working towards a shared values base is an iterative process that is always likely to be emergent rather than definitive. The process of establishing a values-based dialogue is as much a part of community building as is designing the organisational and structural components.

Aims for primary education

1. **Wellbeing:** to respond to every dimension of children's lives – rights, needs, emotional and physical wellbeing, and happiness.

2. **Engagement:** to secure children's active and voluntary involvement in their own education.

3. **Empowerment:** to give young people a sense of personal agency through authentic choice and control.

4. **Autonomy:** to foster a sense of self and awareness of relationships with others.

5. **Respect and reciprocity:** to promote respect for self and others on the basis of mutual regard and courtesy.

6. **Interdependence and reciprocity:** to develop an understanding of the interdependent nature of human society and the natural world.

7. **Local, national and international citizenship:** to develop a strong sense of personal agency through opportunities for genuine choices and active participation as a citizen of school, community, nation and world.

8. **Celebrating culture and community:** to engage in community-based cultural and artistic activities covering a range of opportunities for involvement.

9. **Understanding and making sense of the world:** to understand the variety of ways that humanity makes sense of the world – through moral, spiritual, emotional, aesthetic and physical engagement.

10. **Developing skills:** to build a repertoire of skills rooted in literacy and numeracy, and interpersonal and social skills expressed through the arts and problem solving.

11. **Imagination and creativity:** to develop the confidence to question, seek alternatives, test the boundaries and explore personal potential.

12. **Enabling dialogue:** to develop learning as a social and interactive process based on mutual interaction.

Figure 6: Summary of the Cambridge Primary Review's Aims for Education

Taking part

Developing moral consensus is, as we have seen, very difficult in societies that are essentially pluralistic and individualistic. The values of any society or community are the product of a complex blend of history, theology, philosophy, economics and politics. The moral components of social capital are much simpler where there is a high degree of homogeneity; witness the Amish in Philadelphia, the Orthodox Jewish communities in parts of London, and the historical divide between Catholics and Protestants in Northern Ireland. It takes generations to develop such shared norms, and the polarisation and contradistinction to the rest of a pluralist society serves only to reinforce the exclusive nature of the community.

The process of agreeing the values, passing them on, and reviewing and developing them as necessary over time, means that in terms of community building the process of collaborative engagement with values is as important as pursuing the agreed outcomes. The moral status of any community is almost always a 'work in progress' rather than a definitive and accepted model. For example, issues around ethnicity, sexuality and environmental awareness are likely to be contentious for the foreseeable future, while also pivotal to community development and the enrichment of social capital.

A sense of belonging is fundamental to any debate about the nature of social capital and the reality of how communities actually work. Participation is about being an active citizen, accepting responsibility for the actual working processes of the community, and sharing responsibility for the decision-making that is central to any human enterprise, including leadership in the community. Engagement is about joining in and turning up, being active, and translating the values and vision of the community into daily, lived practice.

Successful communities devote time and energy to celebrating their success as communities. Equally, aspiring communities need to celebrate and so reinforce what it means to be a community. The semiotics of community development are very much concerned with the creation of identity and the shared celebration of common purpose and success.

Citizenship, in the context of social capital, is about commitment to the governance of the community and about accepting responsibility for collective action and accountability. In essence it is about standing for office and voting in elections or referenda. It is about being chair of the trustees of a charity, treasurer of the allotment society, secretary of the friends of the arts festival, and numerous other functions that require individuals to donate time and expertise in order to ensure that things actually get done.

Citizenship is usually defined in terms of rights and duties. Being a citizen implies a range of rights, such as security, residence, voting and legal protection. However, there are concomitant obligations and duties, such as paying taxes, voting and jury service. A key element in any model of community is the way in which those who hold positions of responsibility are held accountable, particularly for the ways in which the principles of the community are translated into consistent practice. It is not totally inappropriate to see it as the management element of communal life.

Significantly, for schools, citizenship has a very clear relationship with democratic principles and practice. In developing the school as a community, it is important that citizenship, and the related practice of democracy, are not seen as another subject but rather as valid and meaningful demonstrations of the practice of democratic communities.

Hubs and networks

We are social animals, but more than that we are at our most effective when we engage with others. Cultural and social capital are largely derived from the quality of the networks that we have access to and the integrity of the relationships that inform their working.

Networks are one of the non-negotiable components of any model of social capital. One characteristic of highly effective people is their ability to network and to systematically build networks.[13] Success as a networker is largely determined by what might be best described as emotional literacy. (Emotional intelligence has been a key concept for a generation,

13. 'Child development is powerfully shaped by social capital ... trust, networks, and norms of reciprocity within a child's family, school, peer group, and larger community have wide-ranging effects on the child's opportunities and choices and, hence, on behaviour and development' (Putnam 2000, p.34)

but there is a strong case for arguing that emotional literacy is a more appropriate term as it implies interaction and relationships rather than a personal quality.)

Networking is fundamental to survival, from the most basic neural networks to the ecology of a forest to human and animal families and finally to complex organisations. Put simply, success in most aspects of life is contingent upon the richness, complexity, depth and breadth of networks. One of the factors that helps in identifying highly effective human beings is the richness of their interpersonal network. The quality of an individual's network is determined by a number of factors, not least of which are emotional literacy and a propensity to live and work in an interdependent way.

Developing the richness and depth of networks is a key function of leadership. In his discussion of social interaction, Alex Pentland argues that:

> Leaders can increase performance by promoting healthy patterns of interaction within their organisations (including both direct interactions, such as conversations, and indirect interactions such as overhearing or observing). (Pentland 2014, p.105)

One of the key challenges of collaboration is the type of leadership needed to achieve what Lasker et al. term 'synergy', or effective partnership. They note that:

> Traditional leaders frequently have a narrow range of expertise, speak a language that can only be understood by their peers, are used to being in control and relate to the people with whom they work as followers and subordinates rather than partners. (Lasker et al. 2001, p.193)

Instead, they identity a need for:

> ... boundary-spanning leaders who understand and appreciate partners' different perspectives, can bridge their diverse culture, and are comfortable sharing ideas, resources and power.

From organisation to community: the building blocks of change

Eric Klinenberg extends the concept of social capital by focusing on what he describes as social infrastructure, which he defines as:

> ... the physical conditions that determine whether social capital develops. When social infrastructure is robust it fosters contact, mutual support and collaboration among friends and neighbours; when degraded it inhibits social activity leaving families and individuals to fend for themselves. Social infrastructure is crucially important, because local face-to-face interactions – at the school, the playground and the corner diner – are the building blocks of all public life. (Klinenberg 2018, p.5)

The importance of seeing the school as a pivotal component of social infrastructure is developed in more detail in Part Four, but it is worth stressing here that people forge bonds in places that have a healthy social infrastructure – a point reinforced by Susan Pinker:

> ... our recent understanding of what drives health and happiness has centred on the concrete ... Now new findings tell us that our relationships – people that we know and care about – are just as crucial to our survival. And not just any kind of social contact, mind you, but the kind that takes place in real time, face-to-face. (Pinker 2014, p.7)

It is the social spaces in the village, not just the village itself, that enable the building of social capital and thus the creation of community. In many ways, the central hypothesis of this book is that the most appropriate model for a learning environment is of a community rooted in the concept of high social capital.

However, schools are currently more likely to be organisations rather than communities, which is understandable when the prevailing orthodoxy in terms of school accountability focuses heavily on the school as an organisational unit. In reality, though, this may well be one of the issues compromising the potential of schools to achieve equity and engagement.

The tensions and issues underpinning the difference between an organisation and a community are summarised in Table 3. There is an obvious danger with tables like this of stereotyping and creating a reductionist caricature. At the same time, it is important to recognise that many of the assumptions underpinning how schools work are often based on a deficit model of social relationships that is essentially negative about human nature.

Organisation	Community
Hierarchical	Team-based
Bureaucratic	Simple systems
Managerialism	Leadership
Top-down communication	Lateral communication
Outcome-focused	Values-based
Control	Trust
Autocratic power	Love
Generic provision	Personalised experiences
Find and fix	Predict and prevent

Table 3: Comparing and Contrasting Organisations and Communities

Elements of both organisation and community are necessary in different combinations at different times and in different circumstances. However, an over-emphasis on organisation has led to an under-emphasis on the need for community in many schools today. And that is a systemic fault as well, not just one affecting individual institutions.

To address this moving forward, we need to start to turn management upside down and start to think about the school inside out. By that, we mean the school consciously needs to build its own strong social capital, modelling community in its daily life. It then becomes possible for the school to radiate this capital outwards in such a way as to positively influence its families and communities, and hence the potential for future educational achievement.

Our discussion of social capital, and how it is built, has highlighted four themes that seem to us to be fundamental in understanding how to make this change possible (see Figure 7). These are the four building blocks of change which have the capacity to help schools unlock the stage beyond school improvement.

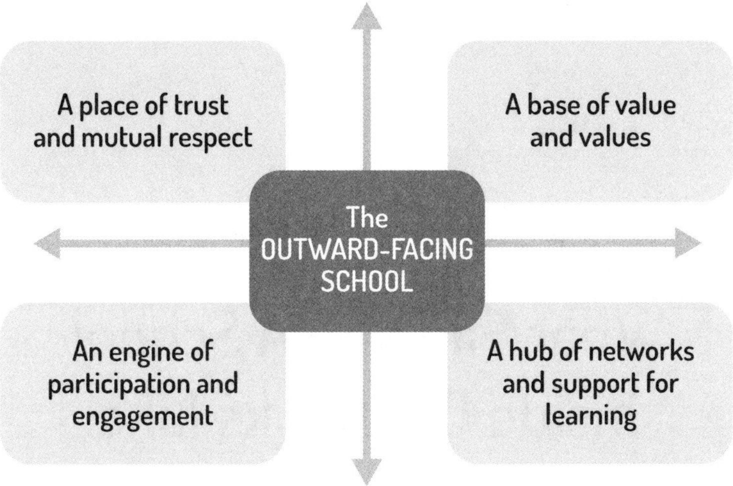

Figure 7: The Four Building Blocks of Change

The key for any school that is looking to flip itself from organisation to community lies in understanding what these four building blocks involve, and especially how they interact in practice, while developing practical strategies that foster their development. In Part Three we will investigate four schools which have started down this road and look at what we can learn from their experience.

PART THREE
What Flipping A School Inside Out Looks Like

Each of the next four chapters is devoted to one of the four building blocks that can contribute to the next phase of school improvement. Each chapter follows a three-part structure which:

- begins with some essential principles, applying the research and theory to the context of education
- explores what those principles can look like in practice through the experience of real schools, and draws key lessons from their experience and practice
- offers some tools and strategies for schools and school leaders who want to take the next steps in their own context.

When we turn anything inside out – a coat or sweater, for instance – we tend to see it as a single action or event. But in reality it is a whole series of smaller steps, such as turning inside out first one sleeve then the other, that add up over time to complete the change. These steps are inter-connected; they are not just linear or fixed in time. And they will be repeated time and again as needed. Likewise, flipping a school inside out to become more outward facing is not a single, simple or an all-at-once act. It is a whole series of adjustments that begin to come together over time to make the change. Our intention here is to open up thinking and awareness about opportunity and strategy, as well as to provide some tools that might aid further local exploration.

For every school, context really, really matters. There is no single blueprint for change. The starting point and pace of change will vary according to context. It is part of the art of leadership to exercise judgement in both, while at the same time cultivating both the capacity and the motivation for change.

Based on our observations of many schools over a good number of years, and our reflections on what we have seen during that time, we have selected four schools for further study – two primary and two secondary schools – that in our judgement have been moving towards inside-out thinking and action. We carried out specific research for this book with each of them in the period from January to June 2019.

This is clearly not intended to be a representative sample. Nor is it intended to suggest these are the only, or even the most highly developed, schools embarking on such change. However, we learnt something important from each one as we spent time with them trying to understand their rationale, intentions and practice, and we will draw on aspects of their experiences to illustrate and explore each of the building blocks in the chapters that follow.

First, though, let us introduce the schools and their contexts.

Goldington Green Academy, Bedford

Goldington Green is a primary academy in Bedford. It serves a varied catchment with a mix of high levels of deprivation and affluent working professionals. It reports significant numbers of families needing support. The proportion of pupils attracting pupil premium is above the national average at 46%, and 26% of pupils have English as an additional language.

The school maintains a strong commitment to values-based education and has a strong focus on diversity and multiculturalism, as well as inclusion. It houses a centre for children on the autistic spectrum on site, as well as a supplementary school for the Polish community.

The school became an academy in 2013 and was rated by Ofsted in 2016 as 'good'. Originally a lower school within a three-tier system of education, after re-organisation it became designated as a primary school, and in 2019 completed its first full primary intake.

Fairfield High School, Bristol

Fairfield High School is an 11–16 school of just over 1000 students, serving an area of high deprivation to the north of Bristol. It has a rich and culturally diverse population, with over 40 nationalities represented within the pupil cohort.

The school, building on the work of its predecessors, has a long history of seeing itself as 'an agent of social change', especially in the period following the St Paul's riots in the 1980s. As a result of a local authority re-organisation of schooling in the area, the school merged with two other schools in 2000, moving in the process to a new building in a different community in 2006. Today it is a member of the Excalibur Multi-Academy Trust.

The Spinney Primary School, Cambridge

The Spinney is a heavily over-subscribed, one-form-entry primary school serving an urban village on the outskirts of Cambridge. It has a diverse intake and around 50% of the pupils speak English as an additional language. Children come from the local estate, built 22 years ago, from the local village community, and from all over the world as their parents take up academic positions at the university or at the nearby hospital.

The school has been judged 'outstanding' by Ofsted twice since 2006. The present headteacher (or 'head learner') has been in her post since 2008. Spinney is an Ashoka Changemaker school, promoting empathy, creativity, teamwork, leadership and change-making. It also leads the Kite Teaching School Alliance.

Homewood School, Tenterden

Homewood School is a very large secondary school and sixth-form centre in Tenterden, Kent. It has over 2000 students and approximately 250 staff. Students attend from a wide area that incorporates urban and rural districts. Most have a white British background and the proportion speaking English as an additional language is below the national average.

Homewood is a non-selective school, but it is situated within the Kent selective system. It gained converter academy status in September 2011 and is described by Ofsted as a 'good' school. In 2011, Homewood was one of the lead schools in the establishment of the Tenterden Rural Alliance – a collaboration with ten local primary schools and one special school. In December 2016, Homewood entered into a more formal relationship with three of its most local primary schools and its on-site nursery school, establishing the Tenterden Schools Trust, a multi-academy trust. Through these partnerships, teachers have worked to deliver cross-phase curriculum projects and joint moderation activities, while sharing in joint professional development.

Although all four of our chosen schools serve quite different contexts and have different histories, there are, interestingly, a number of common features they appear to share:

- An intense focus on relationships.
- An understanding of the importance of values (and of linking these values to the curriculum).
- A deep interest in creativity.
- A certain longevity of staffing and leadership.

We will come across these themes in the chapters that follow, as we draw on the work of each of these schools. Although each school will be used, for the purposes of clarity and simplicity, to illustrate two of our four building blocks, we believe that each school is in fact working on all four fronts, so some overlaps and mutual reinforcement will be evident in each example.

We believe these four examples help to tease out lessons from practice and show how practice, theory and research come together to demonstrate that we can and must start to turn our schools inside out if we are to provide excellence and equity for all our children. Each one offers some important pointers as to how that might be done.

11. The Authentic School: A Place of Trust and Mutual Respect

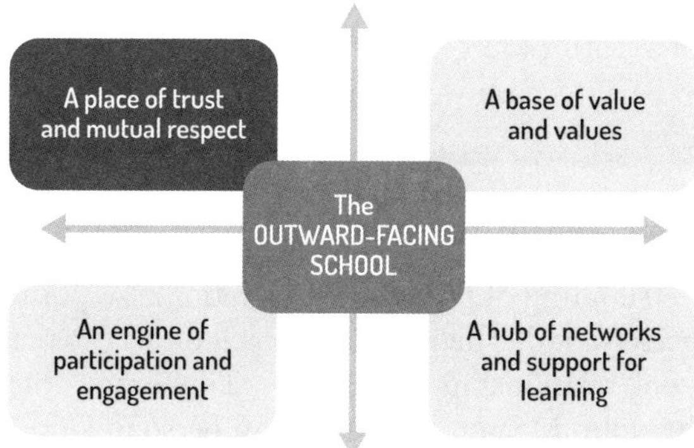

> This is the purpose of education: to foster the growth of loving persons, who are aware both of their individuality and of their membership one of another; who accept one another, and who, understanding their own inter-dependent nature, choose to use their experience creatively in cooperation with one another.
>
> **(Derek Morrell 1973)**

Some principles

These are probably not words that many of us would come out with if asked to explain what schools are for. Nor are they likely to appear in a UK government policy statement any time soon.

Yet the words were indeed penned by a civil servant, the late Derek Morrell, as perhaps indicated by the somewhat formal structure and careful crafting of the language used. The language, too, perhaps gives a clue to its age: the bygone era of the late sixties, a time of 'flower power' and hippies. Morrell's words carry the ring of such a different time and world: one where schools were without performance targets, standard assessment tests, a national curriculum, Ofsted or accountability measures. What possible relevance can his words have to today?

Yet if we ponder the many deep and complex problems our society faces today, it is tempting to wonder how many have their root cause in people's lack of real understanding of their own individuality and of their interdependence with others. And if that were the case, to what extent might it be in part because we have not paid sufficient attention to the purpose of education?

The functional versus the personal

Morrell's understanding of purpose in education also points to a deeper truth about personhood. The identity of each of us as a person exists in and through our relationship with others. This echoes the thinking of the philosopher John Macmurray, for whom personhood:

> ... is constituted by, and does not merely imply, personal relationships between persons. Personality is mutual in its very being. The self is one term in the relation between two selves. It cannot be prior to that relation and, equally, of course, the relation cannot be prior to it. 'I' exists only as a member of the 'You and I'. The self only exists in the communion of selves. (Macmurray 1933, p.137)

Macmurray argues we need to recognise that human beings are deeply situated, communal beings whose personhood is steeped in our relations with other people. He also suggests there are two fundamentally different kinds of relation we have as persons: the functional and the personal.

Functional relations essentially allow people to 'get things done' by treating others as objects and seeing them primarily as a means to an end, for example the assistant on the till when one is making a purchase in a supermarket. Personal relations, on the other hand, are those which view each person as an agent, and which enable people to learn to live in a community.

Macmurray suggests it is important to develop a better understanding of the proper relationship between these two. There is a proper role for functional relations, but this is subservient to the personal. The functional supports the personal; it does not represent an end in itself.

This philosophical perspective on the primacy of personal relations has been increasingly reinforced by advances in scientific and sociological knowledge. For example, in the field of health, the Roseto effect is well known and based on studies of one community, Roseto in Pennsylvania, over a period of 50 years (Wolf and Bruhn 1993). The researchers noticed that heart disease was much less prevalent there than in the nearby, similar community of Bangor. They eventually concluded that mutual respect and cooperation contributed to the health and welfare of a community's inhabitants, and that self-indulgence and lack of concern for others had an opposite effect. They found the characteristics of a tight-knit community to be better predictors of healthy hearts than low levels of serum cholesterol or tobacco use.

More recently, the medical researcher Julianne Holt-Lunstad, looking more broadly at data from 148 studies totalling 308,849 participants, echoed this link between relationships and health (Holt-Lunstad et al. 2010). She concluded that the influence of limited social relationships on mortality risk is comparable with other well-established risk factors, and even exceeds many. In other words, there is strong evidence for a positive correlation between the strength of people's social relations and their health. To quote Stewart Wolf, 'people are nourished by other people' (Grossman and Leroux 1996).

Macmurray's distinction between the functional and the personal and its application to organisations, particularly schools, is further developed by Michael Fielding in a series of papers published from 2000 through to 2012. He suggests the relationship between the functional and the personal in the context of an organisation such as a school can be understood through a four-fold typology (see Figure 8). (Although in a later (2012) version he subsequently adds a fifth type, this does not fundamentally change the model and the simpler version offers greater clarity for our purposes here.)

Schools as **impersonal** organisations	Schools as **affective** communities	Schools as **high performance** learning organisations	Schools as **person-centred** learning communities
The functional marginalises the personal	*The personal marginalises the functional*	*The personal is used for the sake of the functional*	*The functional is used for the sake of the personal*
Organisational type Mechanistic organisation	*Organisational type* Affective community	*Organisational type* Learning organisation	*Organisational type* Learning community
Characteristic mode Efficient	*Characteristic mode* Restorative	*Characteristic mode* Effective	*Characteristic mode* Morally and instrumentally successful

Figure 8: Fielding's Typology of the Interpersonal Orientation of Organisations (adapted from Fielding 2006, p.302)

In the first two modes of Fielding's typology, either the functional or the personal actively excludes the other. In the first case, a predominantly mechanistic organisation is primarily concerned with efficiencies. It is typically dominated by role relations and procedures. In contrast, the second model is animated by an inclusive, restorative impulse, but Fielding notes:

> Its intense concern with the individual needs of young people results in little time or patience for the functional or organisational arrangements needed to translate the warmth and deeply held emotional commitments into practical realities. (Fielding 2006, p.303)

Fielding fairly briskly dismisses both these models as unsuitable for schools because in each, one important element is largely ignored. As a model for any organisation it is therefore incomplete. The third and fourth models in his typology – the high-performance learning organisation and the person-centred learning community – recognise the importance of including both the functional and the personal, but then in fact see the relationship between them in diametrically opposed ways.

The 'high performance learning organisation' is viewed by Fielding as a school dominated by certain kinds of narrow, easily measurable attainments. Students and teachers alike are regarded as being important mainly for their contribution, usually via high-stakes testing, to the public performance of the organisation. Relationships are valued in so far as they serve to promote the purpose of the organisation in the marketplace. In other words, the personal is used for the sake of the functional.

In contrast, in the 'person-centred learning community', the functional is both subservient to the personal and expressive of it. Structures and organisation have within them distinct traces of person-centred ways of being. There is greater emphasis on more participatory, less hierarchical forms of engagement and decision-making, and boundaries between status, role and function are increasingly crossed. More importantly:

> The person-centred school goes beyond the effectiveness of the high-performance model. Its outcomes are widely and imaginatively conceived and its success is as satisfying morally and interpersonally as it is instrumentally. Its form of unity is communal and person-centred, rather than collective and outcomes driven. Its language transcends the bullet point banalities of the effectiveness imperative, celebrating nuance as well as number, delight as well as definition. (Fielding 2000, p.54)

Thus, in the person-centred school, relations between teachers and students, and between teachers themselves, are of the highest quality. The whole environment is designed to enable each student to become a fully developed person in their own right. The outcomes sought are more broadly defined to include personal and social development as well as (not instead of) academic achievement. Easily devolved forms of accountability give way to the 'more demanding, more inclusive notion of shared responsibility' (Fielding 2013, p.7).

Shifting the emphasis from a high-performance learning organisation to a person-centred learning community does not mean that it becomes unimportant how well pupils achieve and attain. This is still an important part of the picture; simply one which, when taken on its own, is too limiting. Rather it is a matter of understanding performance more broadly and enabling pupils to grow towards a full maturity, with a strong personal wellbeing, an ability to understand and shape their own futures, and a clear sense of community.

In this way, by redefining and reshaping its sense of purpose, a school can take its first steps in turning itself inside out. The school that is flipping itself inside out has to begin on the inside, i.e. with the quality and authenticity of the relationships between those inside the school at every level. Otherwise its efforts to influence change outside will be hollow and counterproductive.

In many ways, personhood can be seen as an outcome of social interaction. A relevant concept here is the African idea of ubuntu, which in the Xhosa culture means 'I am because we are'. Or to put it another way: we need other human beings in order to be human. We only achieve our potential for self-actualisation in the extent to which we are able to engage with others. Schooling therefore needs to be understood as part of a process of building personal capacity in order to engage with others. At the heart of this process lies a sense of trust and mutual respect.

For most (but not all) children, their first opportunity to develop personhood lies within their family, and school then represents the opportunity to develop a broader social awareness of community. Of course, for a significant number of children their experience of family is broken or chaotic or both. For them, school represents not just the first but perhaps the only experience of community they have, as well as the only point of stability in their lives. The school therefore has to serve as their model for what living in a community is like. Indeed, this is a school's moral responsibility for all its pupils. That is part of why a school's understanding of the relationship between the functional and the personal matters so much. It is why the first and most important community role of any school is to strive to be a genuine community itself. This will be reflected in its values and in every aspect of its organisation and day-to-day practice.

Developing a sense of belonging

The rise of attachment awareness in English schools has been a comparatively recent trend over the last decade, although the origins of attachment theory in the work of John Bowlby and Mary Ainsworth go back at least another 60 years.

According to Bowlby and Ainsworth,[14] babies develop attachment with their primary caregiver during the first 18 months of life, starting with instinctual behaviours like crying and clinging. Once they reach toddler stage, children begin to develop an internal working model of their attachment relationships, and this provides the framework for their belief about their own self-worth and how much they can depend on others to meet their needs. Secure attachment falls at a mid-point on a continuum of emotion regulation. This is effectively a point of balance between overly organised strategies for controlling and minimising emotions and, at the other extreme, uncontrolled, disorganised and ineffectively managed emotions. This working model, attachment theory argues, also influences the relationships which we engage with in later life. A range of researchers estimate the proportion of children and young people with insecure attachment to at least one caregiver to be between 30% and 40% (e.g. Moullin et al. 2014).

Why does this matter for schools? Rose (2017) argues that an awareness of attachment makes little practical difference for a teacher. He argues that the four main forms of attachment deficit identified by Ainsworth require psychiatric diagnosis which teachers are, inevitably, not qualified to give. Of course, in a technical sense he is right. But it is not the intention to make teachers into classroom psychiatrists, and we would make three points in response.

First, a broad awareness of the causes of behaviour is useful for every teacher. Understanding behaviour and its possible meanings helps to reduce teacher anxiety, while enabling the child to feel understood and to gradually adjust their responses to the classroom and to learning.

14. For an introduction to their work, see for example Ainsworth and Bowlby (1991).

Secondly, although attachment awareness is (rightly in our view) promoted as way to help children and young people who have experienced trauma to have a better experience of school and to develop their personal maturity, in principle that sense of belonging is what all children and young people need. Thinking through what attachment to the school might look like for a child at different stages of their development, and how to secure that, is a key part of building a strong sense of community. A strong community is one which accepts members with problems and looks for ways to support their development. It also adopts strategies to handle divergence and deviance, showing respect for both the individual and, equally, for shared community values.

Thirdly, the notion of attachment also extends to children's families, who need to identify meaningfully with the school so that a sense of shared enterprise, focused on the learning and development of the child, becomes genuine.

Thus there are implications in attachment theory for the school which are not in essence about psychiatric diagnosis. The authentic person-centred school sets out to model community in the way that it chooses to organise itself and to conduct its day-to-day working. This includes accepting the importance of bonding while developing a bridging culture at the same time. Understanding this insight has profound implications, as the evidence of practice helps to illustrate.

Lessons from practice

Wellbeing for all at Goldington Green

Lesson one: values matter, and in the inside-out school everyone needs to live them.

Caroline Skingsley is headteacher of Goldington Green Academy. For her, leading a school is all about 'relationships, relationships, relationships'.[15]

15. All quotes in this case study are drawn from interviews with one of the authors, 24.2.16 and 30.1.19.

She says:

> You have to build the relationships first. Nobody cares what you know until they know you care. When I first came here, we were deemed to be a 'values school'. But I found it was just tokenism. It wasn't embedded. It was just a phrase. So, we actually had to take it right back to the drawing board. Your values underpin everything. In adults, it's our showing each other our values, speaking to people in the way you'd expect to be spoken to, treating them the way you'd expect to be treated. Children will see that being modelled … and in the classroom, you build that same relationship with the children.

And she continues:

> And if you go on to build that relationship with the parent, you won't have the issues and concerns. The parents will know they can approach you if they've got a worry or concern. They're not frightened. You break down the barriers. So, we're constantly looking at how you build those relationships'.

This person-centred approach is then translated into the detail of operational practice, and that means paying special and individual attention to every child, whatever it takes. To give an example, the school has a large and growing number of children with barriers to learning. This includes an increase in the number of families experiencing mental-health issues as well as the number of children needing specific support for mental health and wellbeing. Although there were many strategies in place to support these children, the school noticed it was not really paying attention to what were termed 'quiet children' – those with hidden anxieties or whose families did not necessarily let the school know of significant events that might affect attitudes to learning.

The strategy they put in place sought to build on existing practice to develop a whole-school approach. The starting point was a significant investment in training for all staff at all levels, including two full days on attachment and two on academic resilience.

The curriculum was then adjusted to make sure every child was taught that intelligence is not something fixed for life and that they received training to develop resilience in all aspects of their life.

The school's use of the Leuven scales – a structured methodology for assessing children's levels of wellbeing and involvement – had initially just been confined to the early years, but was developed to become more robust and is now used half-termly with every child across the school. All children with low scores have support put in place, and the school provides its own play therapy and music therapy.

But staff also looked more analytically at the scores to spot where children were developing an atypical profile. As a result, changes that might affect a child's learning were picked up earlier than might otherwise have been the case, with appropriate intervention and support then helping to resolve the difficulty sooner and more easily.

The school also changed its thinking about intervention, beginning to look for and source the right intervention for a particular child rather than trying to fit the child to the intervention. The school also shifted in its understanding of children's priorities. Previously, drawing on Maslow's hierarchy of need (1943), support may have tried to address needs of housing or food first, on the assumption that if these were not addressed then children would not have high wellbeing. The new approach, while still seeking to help with these needs, starts from a different basis, as deputy head Rachel Clay explains:

> We have, as a profession I think, got it wrong in our response to children experiencing barriers to learning. The standard response if a child is struggling learning maths or English has been to give extra maths and English, more of the same. But if teaching is high quality, then the barrier lies elsewhere. So we look for that barrier, and remove it first. And it's often to do with emotional readiness to learn. That's why we've put such hefty investment into training around emotional wellbeing, resilience, and inclusion – to get that right.

Resilience strategies mean that children are not so reliant on teachers, enabling teachers in turn to work differently and more productively.

The change of approach means the school is also now more proactive in securing earlier intervention, leading to an overall reduction in crisis intervention.

Where this requires the support of other agencies, the school has learnt how to ask for what is needed and who to ask, as well as how to build an evidence base to support their case. This has involved a lot of networking, getting to know what particular services offer and named people within each one, and being proactive and persistent in seeking support.

Another key part of the school's strategy is the use of pupil premium funding for a family worker, who is seen as a vital link in providing a friendly and easily accessible face for parents. As well as doing early help assessment, the worker can provide practical support for parents and act as a signpost for advice. As a result, the attendance of specific children has increased, and they have shown both greater progress and stable scores on the Leuven scales.

Becoming a member of the Fairfield Community

Lesson two: a community does not just happen for an inside-out school. It requires care, commitment, work and planning right from the outset.

Pupils joining Fairfield High School in Year 7 participate in an extended, carefully designed and thoroughly thought-through transition programme from their primary schools. This is one significant contributor to the strong ethos and sense of a community that a visitor encounters when entering the school. However, this sense of community has not happened by accident. Pupils do not just arrive at school with that sense. It is consciously built and fostered by the school and, crucially, that effort to secure involvement is also extended to the pupils' families. Creating a strong and vibrant community requires time, commitment, thought, care and planning.

Transition to Fairfield is approached slightly differently for each of the more than 30 primary schools who send pupils, taking account of their circumstances and the numbers of pupils involved. It is, equally, different for each child. In every case, the intention is to gather as much information as possible about each pupil before they come to Fairfield, and for the children to have quality time to visit their new school, to experience the building, environment and ethos, and to become familiar with staff they will encounter.

The process begins in primary school as early as Year 4, two years before pupils are due to move across. All primary pupils, whether or not they are in the Fairfield catchment, can choose to apply for an opportunity to take part in one of the 'Magic Mornings' at Fairfield. These allow them to visit Fairfield and experience two lessons of secondary-school life pitched at a Year 7 level.

At the same time, all Fairfield faculty heads spend time visiting primary schools to see what the curriculum is like, and to make sure Year 7 involves a step up and offers as much stretch as possible for all pupils. One result of this has been to change the structure of Key Stage 3 at Fairfield. Most faculties have dropped their previous Year 8 curriculum to Year 7, Year 9 curriculum to Year 8, and re-drafted their Year 9 curriculum. They had discovered through first-hand experience that the pitch of challenge in their curriculum was based on low expectations of the incoming Year 7 pupils, and they acted in response.

For Year 5 and Year 6 pupils, open evenings are held for the pupils and their families. A key part of this is for pupils and their parents or carers to experience and understand the ethos of Fairfield, and to ensure they want to be part of it. As well as formal presentations, these evenings include an opportunity to talk with staff. Primary school staff also receive an invitation to come and visit, so if they want to build up more of a relationship for individual students, they can.

Fairfield students also run workshops in primary schools for Year 6 pupils, to help make the transition easier. This also provides an opportunity for the Fairfield students to demonstrate their skills and develop their confidence.

Edel Cronin, the assistant vice-principal at Fairfield who is responsible for transitioning, visits every primary school in the summer term to talk with pupils about Fairfield's expectations and what makes it distinctive in terms of its ethos. And later in the term, specific transition days are held to give new students the opportunity to mix with others joining from different schools. A distinctive feature of these transition days is the 'singles and doubles' events held for all students coming from primary schools where there are three or less other students transferring, which give these students an opportunity to bond and mix with others who are in a similar situation to themselves. Meanwhile, the prospective tutors of the new pupils are also being trained at Fairfield, focusing on communication and relationships with families, irrespective of whether they have held the role before.

During the first week of the summer holidays, joining pupils have the opportunity to take part in a summer school, organised by the transition coordinator with the help of an outside provider. Fairfield makes a small charge for this summer school but absorbs the staff costs incurred within its staffing budget. School staff are paid for the extra time they choose to work and all members of staff are given the opportunity to take part, including non-teaching staff. Edel Cronin explains that the reason for this is that 'we want students when they come up to understand that everyone is valued in the school'.[16]

The summer school covers a broad range of activities, ranging from those exploring the communication of emotions to anti-bullying support to science competitions. It ends with a show for parents and carers. Alongside this, and especially to help those who may not have been able to attend the summer school, Fairfield staff have produced a booklet based on a passport of skills which reflect the Year 7 curriculum. These skills and the Year 7 curriculum are linked to free events in the city, which pupils are encouraged to take advantage of in the summer holiday before they transfer.

For example, the Year 7 art curriculum is based around Impressionism, and the booklet encourages pupils to see Impressionist paintings in Bristol Museum for free. The Year 7 history curriculum is based around the establishment of Bristol city, and the booklet pinpoints certain areas of the city to visit.

The passport of skills is seen as important in that it does not continue the SATS treadmill. It means that what students bring into school when they join is not intended or used for test purposes. Its purpose is to help

16. All the quotes in this case study are drawn from interviews with one of the authors 5.2.19

introduce flipped learning in Year 7. Staff hope it will reduce anxiety for students, but they also hope it will help students to see that learning is everywhere, as well as to learn how to disagree with their teachers through giving a valid opinion.

During the first two weeks of starting at Fairfield, all families are invited on a Friday afternoon for tea and cake, while the pupils and their tutors plant a tree on site. The tree is seen as a symbol of growth. Parents then have an opportunity to meet key members of staff informally; usually the parents of about half the year group choose to take up this opportunity.

All Year 7 pupils have the opportunity to participate in building a website (separate from the main school website), which is focused on their transition to Fairfield. It contains videos, photos and blogs based on their experience of the transition process and what it is like to be in secondary school. All primary schools are encouraged to access the website and use it as a tool when they talk with pupils about moving on to secondary school.

Every week the principal, Nick Lewis, invites a group of Year 7 pupils to tea to listen to how they are getting on and to hear their ideas and concerns. What they say is fed back to the senior leadership the following Monday morning. The installation of a PlayPod is one example of how feedback and ideas are picked up and acted on quickly wherever possible.

All of this is possible because Fairfield has a large pastoral team. Each year group has an achievement coordinator and an achievement manager, as well as a link member of the senior leadership team. The school believes that organising in this way (rather than through key stages) makes this broad approach to transition more possible. It is undeniably expensive in terms of staffing and time, at least up-front. There is also a related problem of managing the pressure on primary-school time. The payback comes later on in terms of more secure relationships. Fairfield's approach is also rooted in a belief that academic success is linked to wellbeing. The school is now carrying out research into the impact of its transition strategies. This involves tracking students who did or did not take part in transition events, combined with focus groups of students and parents.

But one instrumental benefit is fairly clearly established. Fairfield is now heavily over-subscribed.

Tools and strategies for building trust and mutual respect

Nel Noddings (1992) argues powerfully that the first job of schools is to care for children. Children do not learn academically if they are not cared for. In other words, their wellbeing is linked to achievement. They need to feel good about going to school.

Bergin and Bergin (2009) highlight the importance of school bonding; of having a sense of belonging at school and a network of relationships with teachers and peers.

> School bonding is akin to attachment in that it can make children feel secure and valued, which can liberate them to take on intellectual and social challenges and explore new ideas. A child who is bonded to school has a sense that 'people at school like me'. A child who is not bonded to school feels lonely, outcast, and alienated. (Bergin and Bergin 2009, p.156)

They go on to suggest a range of actions that teachers in their classrooms and schools as organisations can take to help strengthen school bonding. Some of these are common sense, some perhaps more controversial.

Teachers, they suggest, should look to:

- Increase their sensitivity and the number of warm, positive interactions they have with students.
- Be well prepared for lessons and have high expectations of students.

Both of these are equally important ways for teachers to show they care.

Teachers should also:

- Be responsive to students' agendas by providing choice wherever possible.
- Use induction rather than coercive discipline.
- Help students to be kind, helpful and accepting of one another.

- Implement interventions for difficult relationships in order to repair them.

Then there is a whole-school dimension to consider. Bergin and Bergin suggest school leaders need to:

- Make these approaches school-wide. In other words, all teachers should be consistently positive in their interactions with students.
- Provide a variety of extra-curricular activities, and make sure these are accessible to all students.
- Provide continuity of people and place. Relationships take time, and some research suggests it takes at least nine months for a pupil to become secure with a teacher (Raikes 1993). So it makes sense to minimise disruption through changes of schools or teachers.
- Facilitate transitions to new schools or teachers, using the sort of care and attention to detail shown by Fairfield in their lesson from practice above.
- Decrease transitions in and out of the classroom.
- Keep schools small. It is school not class size that matters; too small a class size may not give pupils enough chance to find a peer buddy. Where schools have to be larger, look at establishing mini-communities within.

In the next chapter, we will consider one example of what this could look like in practice. Meanwhile, perhaps consider just how valued your school makes your students feel. And how do you know?

Once you have formed a view, you may want to make use of the building-block survey tool (Tool 2) in the tools and strategies section of chapter 14 to start to check it out.

12. Towards A Person-Centred Curriculum: A Base of Value and Values

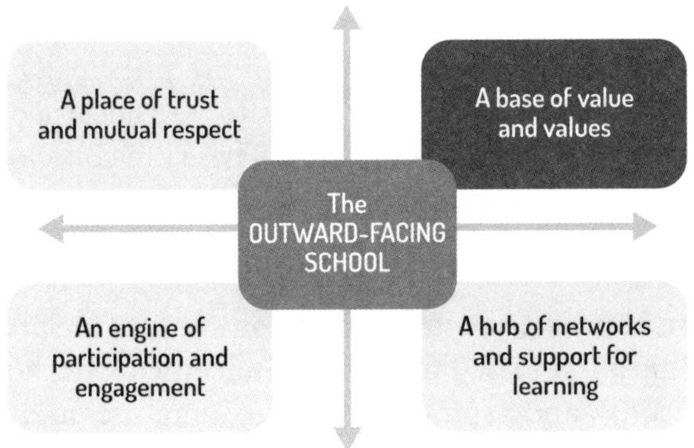

A distinguished Maori educationalist recently told me he was impressed by the way colleges in the UK help people learn how to do things. He was though puzzled by things that they didn't teach: how to be a good family member; how to relate to your community; what stories to tell your children. With an education like this, he wondered, 'Who would want to come to your funeral?'

(Benn 2018, p.63)

When educating the minds of our youths, we must not forget to educate their hearts.

(Dalai Lama)

Some principles

The first of these introductory quotes offers a salutary reminder that what and how we teach reflects the things we value. In doing so, it poses a challenge as to how much importance we really attach to the centrality of relationships. Of course, this does not necessarily mean adding this as a topic to an already overcrowded curriculum. Nor does it necessarily mean that all of this learning has to take place in school, though there is a place for both curriculum review and a greater recognition of the importance of learning beyond the classroom.

In the previous chapter we argued that the quality of the community that a school establishes inside its gates lies at the heart of its role as an engine for building and spreading social capital. But while a sense of community is important, we cannot forget that schools are principally there for the purpose of learning. And learning needs to be concerned with things that matter, that are themselves of value. These are consciously brought together to form the curriculum of the school.

Derek Morrell, who we quoted at the start of chapter 11, argued that:

> The curriculum is a structure erected on a base of reciprocal personal relationships. In curriculum we are concerned with human beings, whose feelings and aspirations are far more real and immediately important to them than the cognitive development which is the educators' stock in trade. (quoted in Drummond 1991, p.35)

Both the academic and the personal matter, but learning is an emotional enterprise and not just a cognitive one, as the Dalai Lama reminded us at the start of this chapter.

A failure to get the experience of school (including the curriculum) right for individuals does not just carry a cost to those individuals. There is also a cost to wider society. One example of this might be the evidence of the comparative failure at school of a significant proportion of the prison population. According to the Surveying Prisoner Crime Reduction report (Williams et al. 2012) – a longitudinal cohort study of adult prisoners sentenced to between one month to four years in England and Wales in 2005 and 2006 – 59% of prisoners stated that they had regularly played truant from school, compared with 5.2% of the non-prison population; 63% had been suspended or temporarily excluded from school; 42% had been permanently excluded or expelled; and 47% had no qualifications (compared with 15% of the working-age population). We might speculate on how many of these offenders could have avoided joining the prison population had there been a way for them feel a closer sense of belonging and fulfilment at school.

The person-centred curriculum

'Personalisation' is perhaps the most commonly used term for an approach to the curriculum that is rooted in individual or personal needs and wants. But it has been much criticised (with justification) on the grounds that it can become impractical when scaled up. At its best, though, it means a structured approach to reconciling generic provision with personal needs and wants.

Despite its difficulties, there are two practical examples of personalisation currently working very successfully in the English school system at the moment: much of early years provision relies on it, as does best practice in special education. In many ways, it is a pity that the principles of early years and SEND learning and teaching are not sustained and spread across mainstream provision.

Those principles may be summarised as:

- Trust the learner's instincts about what they need.
- Respect the perceptions of learners and their parents.
- Work on the basis of personal readiness rather than cohort progression (stage not age).
- Agree the range of required and self-determined topics; for instance, literacy is not optional but learning another language might be.
- Focus on play and socialisation as the foundations for all learning.
- Use formative assessment rather than summative testing.

In essence, personalisation is about negotiating an agreement on what is to be learnt, how it is to be learnt, where and when it is to be learnt, and who will be involved in the learning process. Thus, irrespective of age or ability, the learner is valued and respected on their own terms, and their achievement of their potential is seen as fundamental.

The case for personalisation

One of the issues with the school-centric model is that it has to work in a generic way. It thus inhibits responding to individual needs and wants, often in spite of the best efforts of teachers.

There are three broad arguments in favour of adopting an approach to education that is more personalised:

1. A moral argument based on a belief in the intrinsic right of every child to receive an appropriate education based on their uniqueness and personal needs and wants.
2. A case for a more individual approach to the what and how of schooling that recognises that classrooms and schools at present work on a homogeneous basis when in fact they are highly heterogeneous.
3. An evidence-informed argument drawing on genetic and neurological research to demonstrate that learning, from a scientific perspective, is an individual phenomenon.

The moral imperative for most educators is to achieve the appropriate balance of equity and excellence. There is a very strong school of thought that argues they are in fact mutually exclusive and irreconcilable – that teachers and school leaders have to choose between high excellence and low equity or high equity and low excellence. However, the OECD study *Equity in Education: Breaking Down Barriers to Social Mobility* (2018) identified a number of countries as having both high excellence and high equity. Based on the evidence we offered in Part Two of this book, it comes as no surprise that the highest-ranking countries by this criterion are Singapore, Japan, Estonia, Taipei, Finland and Macao.

The international pattern is also confirmed at a national level: equity and excellence are combined in areas of high social capital. It is clearly unacceptable to have an education system where equitable access to educational success is contingent on, and potentially compromised by, social and economic factors. In spite of the negative perspective that excellence and equity are mutually exclusive, it is possible to combine equity and excellence in education if the social and economic context is geared towards that.

In order to achieve this balance, Charles Leadbeater argued in 2004 that:

> ... we need a new framework to show how personal needs can be taken into account within universal equity and excellence in education. In recent years the policy agenda has grown to recognise the fact that in the context of greater diversity we can only understand these terms by putting the needs and wants of individual learners at the heart of the system. (Leadbeater 2004, p.6)

But his optimism has not been borne out in recent years; in fact quite the opposite has happened in a number of key respects, notably assessment and the nature of the curriculum experience. However, as we will demonstrate, there are still significant opportunities for approaches based on personalisation strategies.

Personalisation and learning

> Possessing different kinds of minds, individuals represent information and knowledge in idiosyncratic ways. (Gardner 1999, p.245)

Gardner's assertion is a fundamental component of any discussion about equity and social justice in education. Reflect on what your answers to the following questions tell you about you as a learner:

- How old were you when you started talking?
- How old were you when you started walking?
- Were there books in your childhood home?
- When did you first read full-length novels?
- What aspects of your primary education remain with you?
- Was the transition to secondary school positive for you?
- How did you cope with the transition to university?

- How would you describe yourself as a learner now?
- Which teacher has had the greatest influence on you?

Now share your answers with a friend or colleague. To what extent are your answers similar and how far are they different?

Now consider your answers to the following questions:

- Which novel has been most significant in your life?
- Which music always makes the hairs on the back of your neck stand up?
- Which films make you cry?
- Who is the greatest athlete/actor/artist of the twentieth century?

Now share your answers with a range of relations, friends and colleagues. What do you think are the chances of someone having the same answers as you?

This is a complex way to make a very simple point. All learners are the product of a wide range of influences and experiences that lead to significant diversity in terms of our life choices and so, too, to our identity as learners. We are all very different, having made countless significant choices that have a cumulative impact on our learning profiles. There is a strong case for developing what might be called a 'learning autobiography' for every child, which develops a cumulative record of all the influences that inform our growth as learners.

This means developing models and a language that enables and supports personal reflection and shared dialogue. Many parents already keep a memory or keepsake box for their young children. It would be useful for families to extend that approach to include evidence of both cognitive and social development,[17] in order to have an evidence base of learning experiences and academic and social development. This holistic view is important because of the existing dominance of narrow and reductionist

17. 'Human caregivers must both fiercely protect each individual child and give that child up when they become an adult; they must allow play and enable work; they must pass on traditions and encourage innovations … There is no simple algorithm to weigh the values of work or play, or of tradition and innovation.' (Gopnik 2016, p.16)

views of what constitutes learning in particular and education in general. Gopnik argues for an integrated and interdependent approach to the curriculum. The act of keeping a learning autobiography has the potential to provide evidence to support learners, parents and carers in actively negotiating both the content of the curriculum and learning strategies to support engagement.

A model of intelligence and its related assessment that focuses exclusively on mathematical, logical and linguistic skills; that many believe is fixed for life; and that can only be measured by crude and narrow quantitative methods is likely to be a barrier to equity and excellence rather than fostering them.

Personalisation: getting started

Personalisation is a powerful strategy in building cultural capital and, crucially, maximising the development of members of the community, irrespective of their age. Personalisation helps to develop the personal resources, skills, aptitudes and qualities that enable us to act.[18]

One approach to personalising learning that has been widely adopted, although not always appropriately, is Gardner's model of multiple intelligences. While there is a very real debate about the nature of intelligence, and varying perspectives on the extent to which Gardner is actually describing intelligences, he does provide a powerful analytical approach that can support review and dialogue and help to develop intervention strategies.

From the perspective of enabling learning to be focused on the individual, current thinking offers two powerful propositions. Firstly, that intelligence is not one monolithic, fixed block, but rather it is a general intellectual capacity (usually described as 'general intelligence') that is amenable to change and growth over time in response to interventions. Secondly,

---

18. 'Developing relationships is a foundation for citizenship, and the large piazzas in the Reggio preschools are seen as important in developing a community and as a microcosm of society paralleling the city piazzas. They are large open spaces where children wander, meet each other, play imaginatively, meet children from other age groups and develop socially.' (Abbott and Nutbrown 2001, p.55)

there are a number of parallel aptitudes and predispositions that describe human potential and educability, underpinned by different techniques and strategies. For example, it is entirely plausible that two people with similar levels of general intelligence will perform very differently in terms of literacy, numeracy, music and sports.[19]

Gardner originally identified seven intelligences; this was increased to eight with the addition of naturalistic intelligence and then to nine with existential intelligence. Gardner has also speculated on the existence of a moral intelligence. Many educators will recognise the nine intelligences as the basis of many models for an appropriate and valid curriculum experience. The nine intelligences cover:

- words (linguistic intelligence)
- numbers or logic (logical-mathematical intelligence)
- pictures (spatial intelligence)
- music (musical intelligence)
- self-reflection (intrapersonal intelligence)
- physical activity (bodily-kinaesthetic intelligence)
- social experiences (interpersonal intelligence)
- an experience in the natural world (naturalist intelligence)
- reflecting on the nature of humanity (existential intelligence).

Now consider the complex profiles of the following people in terms of their multiple intelligences:

- Jacinda Ardern
- David Attenborough
- Malala Yousafzai

19. 'A student's performance on any particular task will depend on both special abilities and general ability, the proportion of each varying from task to task. Such hierarchical models of intelligence, consisting of a general factor plus a number of special factors, have been around for nearly a century and have appeared in various guises.' (Adey and Dillon 2012, p.208)

- Lenny Henry
- Nicola Benedetti
- Steve Redgrave
- JK Rowling
- Martha Lane Fox

It is reasonable to assume that all of these people are highly intelligent in terms of traditional measures (IQ). However, it would be naïve to pretend that their various forms of success are solely attributable to a narrow definition of intelligence; their IQ alone does not help to explain all of the different types of exceptional performance demonstrated in this list.[20]

Linking the personal and the community

One of the key questions in defining the nature of the curriculum is 'Are you a fox or a hedgehog?', which is the title of an essay by Isaiah Berlin that alludes to a proverb attributed to the Greek poet Archilochus: 'The fox knows many things, but the hedgehog knows one big thing.'

In other words, should we aspire to breadth or depth? The answer in terms of personalisation is probably depth with the core learning and breadth with what might be best termed electives. This suggests a defined proportion of time working on the non-negotiables, and the rest of the time following a personal leaning pathway. The ratio between the required and chosen elements is influenced by the needs of the learner and, hopefully, will change over time as the pupil develops and matures as a self-managing learner.

Many primary schools currently follow a pattern of literacy and numeracy in the morning and negotiated topics and projects in the afternoon. Early years pupils are most definitely young foxes. British secondary schools are, by and large, dedicated to creating hedgehogs. Indeed, they are

20. 'IQ measures very general capacities, particularly those that are most important for doing well at school. But having a high IQ or specific kinds of knowledge, such as a knowledge of physics and chemistry is no help when making a soufflé. Wide ranging, flexible and broad learning, the kind that we encourage in high school and college, may actually be in tension with the ability to develop finely honed, controlled and focused expertise in a particular skill' (Gopnik 2016, p.208)

usually run by hedgehogs largely in response to the demands of higher education, which is the natural home of the hedgehog.

Developing cultural capital is about amassing information and building knowledge, but the curriculum also has to focus on skills, behaviours and personal qualities. Therefore, the content of the person-centred curriculum places equal status and significance on knowledge and skills, and on active participation in all aspects of designing the full range of learning experiences.

For many valid reasons, the personalisation of the curriculum is often practically expressed in what is usually described as project-based learning. This is usually based on a challenge or problem-solving approach that requires self-management skills and strategies as well as academic processes. Here are two examples of what can be possible at present.

Example 1

This is an elective course in an American high school, lasting one semester for senior students. In English terms it would be a course for Years 11–13, lasting for at least one term.

Leadership and Community Action

This course is designed to provide students with a comfortable arena to discuss, debate and honestly confront contemporary issues affecting their lives. Topics include cultural diversity, global awareness, healthy relationships, personal identity, school and community culture and climate, stereotyping, substance use, teen violence and teen wellness. Students will receive leadership and issues training opportunities so that they can work as peer educators in the high school and the elementary and upper schools. As a part of this class, students will learn the skills to create and implement a unique project that shows their understanding of the course content and highlights their interests and ideas. In addition to their work in classrooms, the [students] conduct awareness campaigns and host, organise, and design school wide assemblies and conferences ... students are expected to uphold the school motto and reinforce attitudes and behaviours that promote awareness, equity and student engagement. (Cambridge Public Schools 2017)

Example 2

The Middle Years Programme of the International Baccalaureate has a community-service project as part of the compulsory element. This has the following learning outcomes (International Baccalaureate Organization 2016):

- Become more aware of their own strengths and areas for growth.
- Undertake challenges that develop new skills.
- Discuss, evaluate and plan student-initiated activities.
- Persevere in action.
- Work collaboratively with others.
- Develop international-mindedness through global engagement, multilingualism and intercultural understanding.
- Consider the ethical implications of their actions.

These two examples demonstrate the potential for school-based community-focused curriculum provision. Significantly, while they focus on personal development and understanding, they also have a requirement for practical work in the school and the community, thus promoting cultural capital and social capital as well as personal effectiveness and academic qualifications.

Thus a person-centred approach to the curriculum has implications for both its content and its structure. We will explore each through our chosen lessons from practice for this chapter.

Lessons from practice

The totality of experience at The Spinney Primary School

Lesson three: community, values and curriculum are inextricably intertwined.

The curriculum at The Spinney is viewed as the totality of the pupils' learning experience. The statutory requirements of the National

Curriculum are incorporated but they do not dictate the curriculum. According to headteacher Rae Snape, 'we have always done what seemed right for children in front of us'.[21]

The curriculum is underpinned by a clear set of values, which are then translated into pedagogy. Those values are:

- Child-centredness.
- Teamwork and community.
- Excellence.
- Learning.
- Improvement.
- Responsibility.
- Optimism.

Neither the selection of the values nor their implementation is a solitary or single process. They were formed, and are continually refined and tested, through regular, structured professional dialogue and reflection involving all staff. Leadership regularly ensures there is time and space for staff to talk together about the purpose of education. The values are, in the words of Rae Snape, 'lived not laminated'. She continues:

> We enact them as values and sit together to discuss and deepen our understanding of their implications, for instance the implication of valuing optimism in terms of provision for children with special educational needs.

The resulting curriculum is a smorgasbord of elements, encompassing the personal, interpersonal, societal and global. The Spinney curriculum does not fit into easy stereotypes or a single image. The aim is for pupils to be 'happy today, fulfilled in the future, able to work'. The curriculum embraces knowledge, skills and character and sees them as inherently interwoven. The quality of relationships at every level forms the golden thread which binds these strands together (see Figure 9).

21. All quotes from Rae Snape are drawn from interviews with one of the authors, 4.6.19.

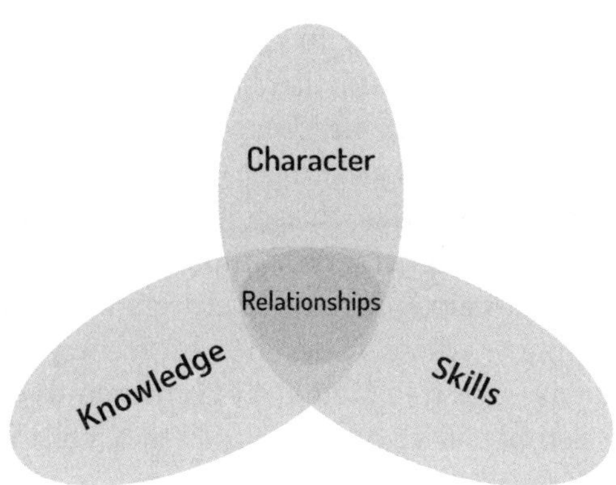

Figure 9: Basis of the Curriculum at the Spinney Primary School

There is a strong emphasis on being able to apply learning to real-life situations. The need to support learning by providing an appropriate context is met, in the main, by organising the curriculum around cross-curricular themes, but discrete subjects are also taught. All of this learning is enhanced by making learning links with other providers and partners, such as The Fitzwilliam Museum, Kettle's Yard and Cambridge University.

The school actively believes that learning is not limited to inside the walls of the school building but can happen anywhere. Therefore, when a learning opportunity arises, staff are encouraged to take advantage of nearby resources and activities. They adopt a 'get on the bus' approach to the curriculum by taking the local bus into the city. Similarly, staff use the outdoor learning environment as much as possible, for example by using the playground and playing field, as well as the adjacent 'Wild Wood'.

The Spinney's teachers believe that children learn better when they are excited and engaged, and so constantly look to provide stimulating and motivating learning opportunities. Importantly, this means thinking creatively – with parents particularly but also with the wider community – about how to use the skills of everyone involved in the school. Visitors and parents are positively welcomed as sources through which the children can extend their knowledge and understanding.

Primary education is a vital stage in children's development, laying the foundations for life. But it should also be a positive, exciting, enjoyable and rich experience for all our children. One of the ways The Spinney has responded to this is by signing up to the Cambridgeshire Creative and Cultural Manifesto for the Curriculum. This is one of a number of examples of integrating research-informed pedagogies into The Spinney curriculum to help ensure high expectations are achieved both in academic learning – where children achieve very strong results in national assessments – but also (and just as importantly) in the prosocial skills and global competencies of communication, collaboration, critical and creative thinking, citizenship and character.

Staff believe that the planned curriculum should be an adventure: a journey of learning undertaken by the children, class and teacher together. The Spinney is an Ashoka Changemaker school promoting empathy, creativity, teamwork, leadership and change-making. Children are involved in planning aspects of the curriculum and contribute to the termly curriculum map. However, this is not seen as pupil voice. For Rae, that term is too hierarchical. She prefers to talk of a 'different but equal' voice.

Underpinning all of the excitement is an equally strong emphasis on structure and discipline. There are very clear routines for children, for instance with regards to leaving a classroom tidy (which is the focus of a routine daily desk inspection). Quirky haircuts, for example, would not be an issue, as in some schools, but all children are expected to wear their team colour. This discipline and its associated expectations derive again from the core values, which the children own and share in the form of the 'Take Five Sustainable Agreements'. These five agreements are sustainable and designed for everyone in the school community. They require pupils to:

- take care of myself
- take care of each other
- take care of my learning
- take care of my school community and world
- take care for the future.

The discipline and expectations also extend to formal learning, though this is often interlinked with personal development. For example, 'Empathy Lab' promotes rigorous skills in reading and writing, but links this at the same time to developing a sense of empathy. During 'Dialogic Literary Gatherings', the children study abridged classical texts (having read an agreed number of pages at home) by sitting together in a circle to discuss the themes in the book. In the 'Big Count', children in mixed age groups solve a set of mathematical problems, with older children acting as mentors and role models to younger ones.

The whole curriculum is predicated on values. It seeks to appreciate and reflect the uniqueness and preciousness of each individual, respecting the dignity of the child and their rights, but understanding this can only happen in balance with a strong sense of teamwork, and with adults modelling the values and learning behaviour that they hope to develop in their children.

The I-College at Homewood School

Lesson four: it is practically possible to make learning both real and personal, even in what might be seen as an orthodox and very large school setting.

Just over six years ago, as part of a whole-school review of pastoral and academic structures, senior leaders at Homewood School began to explore alternative pathways for students. They took the opportunity to consider a specific pathway for students who thrived when given a greater level of independence in their learning. They looked at examples in Finland and Sweden as they formulated an ambition to move away from adult-centred learning, to give more freedom of choice and decision-making to students. The school was already committed to providing different curriculum pathways for students, including the opportunity for practical and vocational learning for some, building on their experience of project-based learning approaches. However, they wanted to take this further.

The opportunity arose with a school re-structuring. The introduction of a new college system led to the creation of what is now called the I-College. The I-College, in the school's own words:

> ... blends recognised teaching methods with independent learning to offer a holistic and rounded curriculum that enables students to become self-motivated learners, who take responsibility for their progress and success.

Today the I-College now takes two forms of entry and has 187 students in Years 7 to 11. But it began much smaller, with just 15 Year 9 students. This incremental approach to radical change has been significant and it has enabled steady progress, which is increasingly evidence-based (though at the outset it needed grounded leaps of faith by senior leadership). Although the I-College has a distinctive pedagogy, it is set up in a way that still enables it to link readily with the mainstream college curriculum. In this way staffing is shared too, and the only additional subsidy the college has required was for the equivalent of one teacher salary in its first year.

In Year 7, students currently study English, maths, science, PSHRE, humanities, PE, French or German, ICT, dance, drama, design technology, art and catering. From Year 9 onwards, it is compulsory for I-College learners to study the following GCSEs: English language and literature, mathematics, and core and additional science. They can also choose to study business studies, geography and statistics. Students then leave the I-College to attend lessons in two elective subjects from within the main school. PE is run as a compulsory programme tailored for the I-College students, and students follow a full PSHRE programme with a bespoke design that allows for a focus on learning, resilience, study styles and time management at key points in the year.

Learning in the I-College takes place in a number of ways. The most recognisable would be the 'Master Classes'. These support conceptual learning through teacher-led instruction, tasks and activities, as would be seen in a traditional lesson. These sessions nevertheless allow time for collaboration and the sharing of thinking and research. Teachers can spend this time evaluating understanding so that interventions and additional support can be provided. The Master Classes may frontload an open-ended task or activity with crucial information or instruction, or provide follow-up conceptual learning following foundation learning or enquiry.

In addition, workshops are independent learning times. These provide opportunities for students to make decisions about how they spend their time and to learn how they learn best. Trial and error and mistakes are encouraged, while teachers aid these sessions by giving feedback and support.

In Key Stage 4, the students make decisions regarding their learning depending on their priorities and deadlines. The workshop sessions are student-directed and led. Students are able to progress and develop independently; tasks can be set by teachers, via Google Classroom, that establish the foundations of learning; while the internet can be used as a resource by students to develop learning, intrigue and depth of thought.

In workshop time, the students are usually engaged in:

- Foundation learning: this is flipped learning whereby students independently learn the basics.
- Collaborative work: embedding learning through short- and long-term activities and projects. These opportunities to work together allow for peer support, and often students can be found at a whiteboard running their own Master Class, or students will coordinate themselves to read English literature texts. Students may also spend this time completing conceptual tasks, allowing them to study subject content in depth and to develop skills of extended writing, analysis and evaluation.

At the start of Year 7, teachers have control over how workshop time is spent, but over the course of Years 7 and 8, sessions are added to the timetable and open-ended tasks are set. These enable students to make decisions about how they should spend their time in readiness to be most effective in Year 9 onwards.

In Years 10 and 11, each student has an allocated desk space which they personalise for themselves. Such ownership is designed to prompt both accountability and responsibility.

Within the I-College there are breakout areas for Master Classes, which resemble a traditional classroom space; group work areas for collaboration and peer support, where seating and table areas resemble a common room; and independent learning spaces housing students' allocated desks. Learning skills are developed through a fine and individual balance of teacher-led and student-directed time that flexes and evolves over the course of five years. Open-ended tasks are introduced in Year 7 and their use developed over time to ensure that students manage themselves to meet deadlines, so they are able to hand in quality outcomes that reflect their best abilities.

'Learning Coaches' are crucial members of the I-College teaching team. They are assigned students who they meet with once every two to three weeks. Their objectives are to:

- Support students in self-reflection and target setting. Various tools and techniques are used and adapted to suit the needs of each student.
- Facilitate students in their planning and time management. Sometimes this may involve helping to plan a student's diary for the week or reviewing deadlines coming up.
- Use questioning techniques to enable students to take responsibility for their own learning and progress. Students hold themselves accountable for their own targets. This is enabled because the students set these targets for themselves in the first place, and such ownership supports accountability.

The learning coaches also monitor the students' work rates and quality of outcomes, coordinating interventions or further challenge as needed. Coaching prompts intrinsic motivation and enthusiasm for learning. Constant review and self-reflection, together with the celebration of success and personal accountability, powerfully encourages learners to do it for themselves. The aim is to educate the whole child, as opposed to delivering a series of subjects – and to ensure robust and timely interventions are put in place early on, as opposed to troubleshooting in the year of exams – through:

- embedding a culture of higher-order thinking, drawing on Bloom's taxonomy and the theory of growth mindset
- instilling high expectations for work rates and outcomes for all.

Student leadership also has an important place in the I-College. Year 10 'Peer Mentors' are allocated to Year 7 and 9 students. They take this role very seriously and the younger students can often be found seeking out their peer mentor when they need them. The college has a senior head boy and girl in Year 10 and a junior head boy and girl in Year 7. They represent the I-College at events such as open evenings or visitor tours. All students are encouraged to suggest and run with ideas that they may have, with many organising initiatives to fundraise or improve their learning opportunities. Finally, due to its inherent flexibility, the college is able to offer facilities and student peer support for afternoon activities to partner primary schools. This has in turn started to help build I-Learning into the Key Stage 2 curriculum.

A number of key ingredients have had to come together to make the I-College development possible: notably leadership and commitment, combined with a sensitive persistence to overcome initial reluctance.

Kate Farrell has been the driving force behind the college from its inception.[22] She says the prime requisites for success are to:

- have a committed headteacher who champions the work
- have a thick skin or strong armour
- not expect too much too soon
- maintain a steady process (she has had a five-year plan to build a team to support the programme)
- stay very flexible
- build relationships with people (but understand you won't win everyone round)
- support teachers through change with individual coaching.

But above all, she advises any leader contemplating moving towards a more person-centred curriculum to 'just to do it – it is both very rewarding, and very necessary'.

---

22. All quotes from Kate Farrell are drawn from interviews with one of the authors, 9.4.19.

Tools and strategies for creating value and values

1. Learning to learn

Central to personalising learning is the development of confident, self-managing learners who are self-motivating and comfortable with working reflexively and metacognitively.

The Education Endowment Foundation's report *Metacognition and Self-Regulated Learning* (Quigley et al. 2018) points to a number of evidence-based strategies to enhance the potential contribution of metacognitive approaches. The report argues that teachers should acquire the professional understanding and skills to:

- develop their pupils' metacognitive knowledge
- explicitly teach pupils metacognitive strategies, including how to plan, monitor and evaluate their learning independently
- support pupils to plan, monitor and evaluate their learning
- promote and develop metacognitive talk in the classroom
- set an appropriate level of challenge to develop pupils' self-regulation and metacognition.

Schools should also support teachers to develop knowledge of these approaches and expect them to be applied appropriately.

There are numerous alternative models that describe the cognitive resources, strategies and skills that learners need in order to become confident in managing their own learning. An example can be found in Table 4.

Directly related to the cognitive skills and strategies are their parallel social or relational skills, as illustrated in Table 5. The two strategies need to be seen as interdependent and mutually inclusive.

What is important about both sets of skills and strategies is that they are not treated as separate entities, but rather are seen as dimensions of personal wellbeing and effectiveness. It is very important that they do not become subjects that are taught and assessed, but rather are seen as a means to take control and have the confidence to make choices. It might be helpful to see them as a toolkit that offers a range of appropriate resources, where it is as important to know when and how to use the various components as it is to be confident in knowing about them.

Strategies	**Applications**
Literacy and numeracy	• Reading for understanding • Confidence with abstract concepts • Critical reading • Survey, question, read, recite, review (SQ3R) • Note taking • Précis
Communication	• Oracy • Written • Multi-media
Cognitive strategies	• Memory/recall • Practice • Concentration/focus • Intrinsic motivation • Resilience • Growth mindset • Creativity • Problem solving
Intellectual skills	• Research skills • Analysis • Explanation • Justification • Testing hypotheses • Compare and contrast
Metacognitive approaches	• Reflection and reflexivity • Monitoring and review • Self-assessment • Peer review

Table 4: Learning to Learn – Cognitive Skills and Strategies

Strategies	Applications
Wellbeing for learning	• Creating a learning space • Time management • Rest, diet, exercise • Play
Interpersonal literacy	• Sensitivity to impact on others • Responding to body language • Adopting and adapting
Intrapersonal intelligence	• Reflection and reflexivity • Understanding and regulating their own emotions • Self-awareness
Trust	• Openness • Disclosure • Confidence • Delegation
Cooperation	• Teamwork • Collaborative working • Building consensus
Empathy	• Sensitivity • Respect • Inclusion • Compassion • Kindness
Listening	• Feedback • Attending • Mirroring and echoing
Resilience	• Engagement • Commitment

Table 5: Learning to Learn – Social and Personal Skills and Strategies

2. Why not a personal learning plan?

Personalising the curriculum can also draw on a range of successful strategies, experience and skills derived from the usage of Individual Learning Plans (ILP) or Individual Education Plans, which are commonly developed for pupils with particular special needs or disabilities.

The ILP is essentially a contract and as such has to be managed according to the following principles:

- The starting point for an ILP is a review and diagnosis of the pupil's needs, interests and development.
- The review is followed by a negotiation of the individual's learning priorities, dispositions and the content of their curriculum.
- This process is a dialogue involving the pupil, their parents or carers and appropriate staff, who work collaboratively to determine specific targets for the pupil and to agree how these will be reached.
- The ILP allows staff to plan for progression, to monitor the effectiveness of their teaching and to identify the need for additional support.
- The ILP includes details of assessment and how the plan will be monitored in order to ensure outcomes are achieved and future progression is managed.
- The plan should include reference to the possibilities for learning at home and across the community, collaborating with parents and other members of staff to help the child become more involved in their own learning and to work towards specific targets.

The ILP should be a formative document and reviewed regularly to ensure that it continues to be relevant and fit for purpose. When reviewing the ILP, teachers need to engage with the views of both the pupil and their parents or carers. The review should consider the progress made by the pupil, any specific issues that impact on the child's progress, and any changes to targets or strategies.

Would not every learner benefit from some form of ongoing ILP?

13. Breaking Down Barriers: An Engine of Participation and Engagement

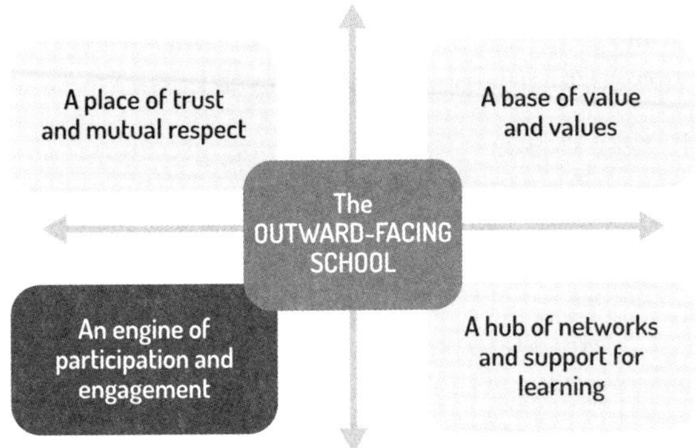

Some principles

There is a sense in which education is everyone's business. Not only has everyone been through some form of educational system (most commonly the school system, for a minimum period of time), but everyone is also affected by the outcomes of other people's education. In addition, schools themselves directly influence, to some degree, both the economic and social environment for us all, at both a local and national level.

This manifestly does not make everyone an expert on education. However, nor does it mean that schools can be fully effective as educators without the active participation of their key stakeholders. For instance, no-one can be educated against their will, and school takes up a significant portion of childhood and adolescence. In chapter 8 we saw the crucial role played by the family in supporting educational achievement. The community reasonably wants to know that it is receiving a return on its investment in schooling. All have an important stake in a school.

Despite this, the most common default position of schools in the past has been to seek, above all else, a degree of compliance from their stakeholders. The child and the parent are recipients of an educational process handed down to them. While it is assumed the community has had some stake in shaping this through the voices of their politicians, beyond that they are often no more than passive observers, and indeed encouraged to be so to a significant extent.

Each of these three key stakeholders – parent, child and community – has legitimate expectations for schooling that go beyond mere compliance, as well as an important contribution to make to the success of schools. Yet each group also faces barriers to effective engagement.

Understanding participation and engagement

There are numerous synonyms for participation and engagement, all of which point to varying degrees of commitment or engagement. For example, 'consultation' is often used in place of 'participation', where in fact it actually describes a limited and partial form of participation. There will always be degrees of participation and engagement according to a range of criteria, and the level of involvement is a key factor in determining the level of social capital and cultural capital.

One way of differentiating participation and engagement is to think of different modes of commitment, with participation as the public expression or interpersonal aspect and engagement as the subjective or intrapersonal expression. The cultivation of both can be directly related to extrinsic and intrinsic motivation theories respectively. As is often the case, intrinsic and extrinsic strategies have to be seen in a symbiotic relationship, with an external outcome only being valued to the extent that it is a) worthwhile and b) attainable.

A significant but often ignored component of cultural and social capital is the propensity and potential to act. One of the problems with utopian models of community is that they rarely acknowledge social and economic realities (how to translate their often worthy vision for the future into relationships, structures and outcomes). Equally, cultural capital requires the balancing of the ability to envision a preferred future with a range of personal attributes, not least of which is the ability to be proactive in the pursuit of an ideal future state.

A key factor in understanding participation and engagement is the potential for personal and collective agency. In this context, agency is seen to have some or all of the following characteristics:

- The ability to see the relationship between principle and practice, aspiration and implementation.
- The capacity to make significant and valid choices while acting independently.
- The confidence to interpret situations and make valid and consistent moral judgements.
- The ability to manage the practical implications of choices made in terms of resources and relationships.

Underpinning each of these characteristics is access to, and confidence in the use of, the language of any given community. One of the most pernicious manifestations of social class is the use of literacy as a means of regulating social mobility. A key indicator of cultural capital is the ability to adopt the specialist vocabulary of the wider community. Levels of participation and engagement are significantly determined by confidence and fluency in the language used by appropriate groups and sub-groups. This in turn informs and influences self-efficacy as well as cultural and social capital.

Participation in principle

Virtually all organisations, and most communities, relate the degree of participation to some form of hierarchy. On the basis of a range of criteria, sometimes explicit but not always, individuals are able to understand their place in a hierarchy that is usually based on their level of authority to act, their access to different types of information, and their ability to take various types of decision.

The reality of participation in schools and other organisations depends on the extent to which significant numbers of stakeholders are on the right-hand side of Figure 10. Clearly the range for control to subsidiarity will vary significantly according to a wide range of criteria, partly practical and partly moral. Thus, pupils may have a school council that discusses charitable activities, aspects of uniform and school meals. But they are not able to discuss the most significant factors – the quality of teaching and learning, and curriculum choice. Participation may therefore be said to be largely symbolic and ritualistic. Equally, teaching staff are often involved in participatory activities on a need-to-know basis determined by senior staff.

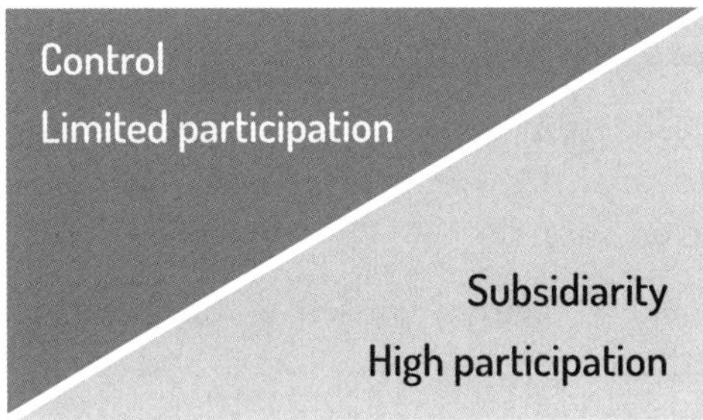

Figure 10: The Balance of Control Versus Subsidiarity

The importance of personalising learning (as discussed in chapter 12 with regards to Homewood School) is another example of degrees of participation, with a very wide range of examples of practice found across the same school. One of the criteria for a successful community based on high social capital is a culture of openness and transparency. This implies high levels of participation, not by virtue of seniority or longevity but rather by virtue of membership of the community, irrespective of status.

A significant endorsement of the importance of participation with one group of key stakeholders – teachers – is found in the collective teacher efficacy model promulgated by Eells (2011) and cited by Hattie and Zierer (2018, p.26). Eells' synthesis of a range of research projects identified collective teacher efficacy (CTE) as pivotal to student achievement, with an effect size of 1.23 (where an effect size of 0.4 is usually regarded as being significant in terms of validity and reliability and so a basis for evidence-informed action).

CTE refers to a staff's shared belief that, through their collective action, they can positively influence student outcomes, including those who are disengaged and/or disadvantaged. There is a very high correlation between CTE and high social capital. Educators with high efficacy:

- show greater effort and persistence
- are willing to try new teaching approaches
- set more challenging goals
- attend more closely to the needs of students who require extra assistance.

Key factors in achieving collective teacher efficacy are:

- Advanced teacher influence: this is defined by the degree to which teachers are provided opportunities to participate in important school-wide decisions.
- Goal consensus: reaching consensus on goals not only increases collective efficacy, it also has a direct and measurable impact on student achievement.
- Teachers' knowledge about one another's work: teachers gain confidence in their peers' ability to impact student learning when they have more intimate knowledge about each other's practice.
- Cohesive staff: cohesion is defined as the degree to which teachers agree with each other on fundamental educational issues.
- Responsiveness of leadership: responsive leaders show concern and respect for their staff and protect teachers from issues that detract from their teaching time and focus.
- Effective systems of intervention: effective systems of intervention help in ensuring that all students are successful.

A number of key themes emerge from this model: involvement, consensus, transparency and responsiveness. These can be seen as pivotal leadership behaviours that have a significant influence in terms of developing engagement. Although CTE is very much rooted in the participation and engagement of teachers, it is worth considering its potential as a model that, with adaptation, could inform working with students and their parents. Some possible tools to support this are included at the end of this chapter.

Engagement in principle

Engagement is fundamental to educational success. In many respects the ideal student is one who has high engagement over time. Engagement is also a highly significant element of cultural capital, in that high cultural capital equates almost exactly with the nature of engagement as defined by the Cambridge Primary Review: 'to secure children's active, willing and enthusiastic engagement in their learning' (Alexander et al. 2010, p.197).

This is a noble aspiration, but it immediately calls into question our confidence that what is being provided is actually fit for purpose in terms of the curriculum being offered and the learning experiences being made available. Learning has to be capable of inspiring those engaged responses. This also takes us back to the issue of personalisation and the need to move away from school-centric towards learner-centric education. Too often, engagement by pupils is seen in terms of being present and behaving in prescribed ways. Sometimes the same principles are applied to teachers and parents!

The most significant components of pupil engagement may be summarised as follows.

- Attendance: this usually means attendance at school, but surely it should be redefined to include learning in the home and the community. That is why we feel a nagging concern about fining parents for missing the last week of the summer term, when those children could have time devoted to their family with a wide range of learning activities together.
- Behaviour: there is a worrying tendency to see compliance with strict (or even draconian) rules as good behaviour, when in fact it

is control based on obedience and conformity. Behaviour should be about courtesy and mutual respect that is based on genuine reciprocity. Courtesy, as opposed to obedience, is a basic element of cultural capital.

- Basic skills: engagement requires a portfolio of skills and learning strategies in order for the pupil to actually be able to participate. The most obvious of these are oracy and literacy. There is a very high correlation between a lack of engagement and low levels of literacy. Engagement also requires cognitive skills, notably problem solving and risk assessment, time-keeping, concentration and the ability to manage anger and frustration. Those who are successful in educational and social terms tend to have these skills in abundance and so secure their cultural capital.
- Opportunities for success: the most vulnerable and marginalised young people are the least likely to succeed according to most of the prevailing norms. It is difficult to imagine what it means to fail in most lessons, on most days, for most weeks and terms. Habituated failure is one of the most negative indicators of failure to engage and low cultural capital. This is not to advocate 'prizes for all', but rather to recognise that the world is not as neat as a secondary school timetable, nor as potentially individually appropriate as a primary school curriculum. Engagement has to acknowledge and respect difference, and that includes alternative definitions of success.
- Wellbeing: engagement implies physical and mental health. Without a sense of personal wellbeing, it is difficult to envisage the sort of commitment that comes from a balanced diet, regular exercise, a lack of stress, and a sense of optimism and hope based on an ability to articulate a preferred future. Engagement in learning presupposes physical and mental wellness, the absence of hunger, opportunities for pleasure and enjoyment, and a rich network offering care, support and love.

Participation and engagement in practice

In spite of some compelling evidence that suggests otherwise (both research-based and anecdotal), securing participation and engagement is much more difficult than it would appear. This is mainly due to the social context of the school. There are a range of barriers that can inhibit or compromise attempts at promoting participation and engagement.

Not all of these barriers are caused by the school. People legitimately have other matters to attend to: childcare, work, friendships and so on. Moreover, the nature, level and extent of any involvement will legitimately vary with time and circumstance. However, barriers to engagement can sometimes be wittingly or unwittingly created or reinforced by the school.

Taking down the barriers is the key to making engagement real. It forms an essential element in flipping the school inside out. Let us look in more depth at each stakeholder group in turn, the challenges they face, and how these challenges might be overcome.

Parent engagement

Janet Goodall (2018) argues persuasively that school leaders are in the grip of superstition about parental engagement. By superstition, she means something we believe because, in essence, we do not know any better: something that is believed without evidence, and something many (but not all) believe and therefore few argue against.

Recognising the importance of parental engagement, schools interpret this as needing to 'get parents in', especially those that are seen as 'hard to reach'. This means, most often, coming to a meeting in the school. At that meeting, parents can be told by a teacher how their child is doing and perhaps advised what they can do to help their child perform better at school. Or in other words, to help the teacher do their job.

Goodall's argument is that while this may have a place, its importance is at best secondary. The real focus of school-parent interaction should be on how schools and parents can together best support children's learning, much of which does not happen in school.

Steven Constantino (2015) suggests the problem is reciprocal. Parents are afraid of schools and teachers are often afraid of parents, because both sides have had poor experiences of the other at some point. Families fear they cannot deal with the complexity of the school or be seen as equal. School staff fear family reactions to school information or happenings. This leads to a reciprocal lack of trust, which can be further fuelled by the school through such factors as poor or one-way communication or the lack of a welcoming environment. These are the type of barriers that need to be removed.

A school which is setting out to engage with parents as partners in learning recognises parents as the primary educators of and 'experts' on their own children. Such a school also knows that children and young people learn best when what they learn is mutually valued and reinforced at home and at school.

We think such a school needs to develop five key characteristics, all of which require a whole-school understanding and professional development for all staff:

1. The school is open and welcoming

This includes attending to the physical environment, the language and style of communications, the attitude of staff, and being both responsive and inclusive.

2. The school communicates clearly and frequently with parents

This includes listening and establishing dialogue with parents in non-threatening ways, and it means having an awareness of parents' needs (which is developed by exploring their needs without making assumptions).

3. The school responds flexibly to parents' needs and circumstances

It is confident and approachable, takes time to get to know people as individuals, seeks to understand parents' perspectives, and takes a constructive attitude to complaints and criticism.

4. The school encourages parents as educators and learners

It believes that all parents are interested in their child's education (regardless of any evidence to suggest otherwise), and takes special care to explain to parents how they can support their child's learning. It systematically exchanges information with parents about the curriculum and their child's progress, and takes the initiative to keep the gate open.

5. The school strengthens the voice of parents in the school

It is proactive in its approach, acts early to gain parents' involvement, finds ways to enable less confident parents to participate and contribute, and shows parents their voice makes a difference. It develops the confidence of staff to respond and engage productively with parents. Yet it also remains aware of all stakeholders (not just current parents).

Student engagement

As far back as 1964, Paul Goodman suggested that many young people react to the strictures of schooling with 'reactive stupidity' (Goodman 1964). Students either disengage from the system or begin to act out the anxieties, fears and anger that have been denied and repressed by the system. He suggests the ultimate end of the educative process should be enhancing the ability of young people to act wisely and well, on their own initiative.

Traditionally, our understanding of youth leadership has been influenced by research conducted by and with adults. Young people are rarely seen as a source of valid and valuable insights into leadership development and its practice. They are often perceived as not mature enough. This views young people as recipients rather than active partners in leadership development and school improvement.

It is only comparatively recently that this view has begun to be challenged in practice, and some researchers doubt that a significant shift in the relationship between school and young people is possible due to the inherent power imbalance. However, programmes such as Learning Ambassadors, developed by Schools of Tomorrow, may have begun to redefine some of those boundaries.

Learning Ambassadors are trained students who focus on supporting the improvement of teaching and learning within the school, through observations and interviews with students, providing feedback to teachers within a carefully structured framework. Meanwhile, other models, such as Student Action Teams (developed by Roger Holdsworth), focus on students leading change within the community beyond the school.

Student Action Teams are groups of students who work on a real, identified issue of community interest. The students carry out research on the topic and develop solutions, either as proposals for others or actions they can then take themselves. Holdsworth argues there are changed roles for students in their learning through such teams (Holdsworth 2011). Learning is:

- purposeful: students see outcomes that are important to them
- productive: students create something that makes a difference
- communal: students work together with fellow students, teachers and others.

It is important to recognise that there are degrees of involvement and participation, which affect how far young people are genuinely engaged in what they are doing. The 'Ladder of Participation', originally outlined by Roger Hart in the early 1990s, has been widely used and adapted by teachers and others, particularly in relation to the development of student voice approaches (Hart 1992). The 'eight rungs' that he suggests imply a sequential progression of stages that increasingly involve young people, with young people being 'manipulated' at rung 1 to 'young people and adults sharing decision-making' at rung 8. We think that is a somewhat simplistic model of how participation develops in the real world.

Hart himself has criticised the way the ladder has been used and interpreted by others. He concludes that 'the important distinction … is how the children think of themselves and the adults'. So, at 'the top of the ladder', children:

> should not be 'children in charge' but children as citizens who think of themselves as members of a larger community that includes adults and other children who they may sometimes invite to join them. (Hart 2008, p.29)

For Hart, engagement with others is a key distinction that recognises the difference between collectivist cultures and those that emphasise individuals. We would further criticise the notion of a simple hierarchy and linear progression implicit in a ladder model in favour of understanding progression as more akin to a spiral or a matrix of opportunity.

Groves et al. (2015) conclude that, in developing learners of and for the future, we need to ensure that students are not just involved and engaged, but also able to exercise agency. The exercise of agency, in any context, is challenging to existing authority. It offers different opinions, asks questions, and suggests different solutions. The exercise of agency inevitably means that people are no longer willing to be compliant, not because they wish to disagree and oppose, but in order to work together to learn, be creative, share in the excitement of exploration, and find better ways forward.

Community engagement

Catherine Hands, in a qualitative study of two Canadian schools, found numerous possible benefits of wider partnerships for schools:

> Partnerships with community organisations and citizens not only provided students with academic resources and additional learning opportunities, but expanded students' networks and increased their social capital. By meeting and interacting with citizens in their community, students developed relationships and subsequently had access to information, learning and occupational experiences, and opportunities to establish trustworthiness. Partnerships also promoted an awareness of the need for community participation among students. (Hands 2010, p.203)

That is an impressive list of benefits, which serves to remind us that not all important learning by any means happens in school. Carefully structured opportunities to learn in the community beyond the school can play an important developmental role for young people. However, the school has an important part to play in making that possible.

We might add to the benefits mentioned above the potential for the school, and indeed the wider school system, to benefit from fostering a deeper shared understanding of purpose between the wider community and the school.

One example of the power of community engagement is provided by the Edge Foundation (2019), which has researched how countries other than the UK are meeting the challenges posed for education by the modern world. Their investigation took them to Nashville, Tennessee.

In 2005, the city of Nashville had a high-school graduation rate of just 58% and businesses were not getting the skilled individuals they needed. In the words of Melissa Jaggers, President of Alignment Nashville, 'we knew it wasn't time for tweaks, it was time for wholesale change' (Edge Foundation 2019, p.11). That is exactly what they embarked on, led by the business community in partnership with the school board. They focused on making learning relevant to real life and involving employers and the community, as well as training teachers in this new way of working.

The transformation was supported by Ford Next Generation Learning. Ford NGL is an experienced and respected US-based non-profit, created by the Ford Motor Company Fund, that has developed a community-driven approach to educational transformation based on the use of community engagement to advance student, community and workforce success.

As a result, high-school attendance rose from 87% to 96% and suspensions fell by 40%, as young people felt more engaged. In ten years, the graduation rate went from 58% to 81%, with significant improvements in students' grades. Given the average difference in annual income between a high school drop-out and high school graduate, it is estimated that more than 12,200 additional students have graduated, adding more than $100m to the local economy every year.

To achieve such benefits, and to effectively transform the way that schools prepare young people for life and work in the twenty-first century, the research literature[23] is clear that learning institutions need to engage in and facilitate dialogue between school staff, leaders, pupils and parents, governors, employers and community organisations.

23. See for example Mann et al. (2018) and Mann et al. (2017).

Lessons from practice

Engaging communities at Goldington Green

Lesson five: to be willing to engage, people need to feel wanted and that their engagement will be of value in some way, and to see a reason for doing so.

Engagement is not about a single act or initiative. It is more a state of mind. It is about many strands of small, mutually reinforcing actions and activities tailored to circumstance and need; a continuously changing and shifting pattern of interactions between groups of people who share some common interests and some which diverge. As always, it begins (and ends) with the pupils.

The Heritage Bag project was launched at Goldington Green to enable all children to share their family heritage, traditions and culture. The idea is that the school provides a heritage bag with simple prompts and ideas tailored to each year group's curriculum. Every child has the opportunity over the course of a year to take the heritage bag home and add information to it about their family's heritage; each year the bag takes a different form in terms of the prompts and ideas that accompany it.

In this way parents may begin to engage. The purpose of parent engagement is not fundamentally to ensure parents support the school in its work, but for the school to help parents to best support their children's learning. For Goldington Green, that means building on the school's central focus of relationships and core values.

This does not involve some romanticised, rose-tinted view of people. It means being aware of the challenge of different cultures, and the fact that people will disagree but also have much in common. It recognises that to be engaged is also about taking your share of responsibility. A schools' relationship with parents is complex and multi-faceted.

In a development of the Heritage Bag project, a group of Polish parents worked closely with a local artist to create personal suitcases. These included lots of interesting and memorable items such as their family trees, objects from their ancestors and plenty of wonderful photos of members of their families. The parents went on to share their findings with their children so that all can celebrate the importance of knowing where they come from. The impact was high. The project sparked a shift in behaviour, moving these Polish parents (who had felt they were not able to join the school's bonfire night celebration) towards active acceptance and involvement as part of the school community.

As its Polish community grew, the school agreed to lend premises for a supplementary school run on Saturdays by the Polish Cultural Centre. The supplementary school was offered a reduced rent and in exchange it provided trained workers to liaise between the schools and new families arriving, so as to build a relationship from the outset.

The school has found that two very powerful levers for building relationships that result in engagement are the arts and food. Both are about opportunities for sharing in a threatening environment, and both strongly reflect cultural identity.

Goldington goes out to meet people where they are as much as it invites people in. The school arranges coffee mornings for personally invited parents in Tesco's or the local pub, led by two members of the support staff. At Christmas, parents are invited into classrooms during the day to make decorations with their children.

Because the school can appear a threatening place for many, a wooden summer house was acquired and placed in the school grounds. A local grandmother who used to work at the school regularly holds drop-in sessions there for parents, which may vary from learning some needlework to providing an opportunity to chat about parents' concerns, such as worrying that their children are not sleeping well. The local grapevine is used to spread the word about these drop-in sessions.

The strong ethos and culture of mutual respect that the school actively fosters means pupils are also able to have a voice. At a formal level there is a school parliament. Every class elects its own MP to the parliament, which meets each week with the deputy head. Both staff and pupils can, and do, refer matters to MPs where they think something connected to the school can be improved. Less formally, a 'listening box' provides a place where children can leave messages to share a problem with an adult, if they don't feel able to raise it directly.

Other opportunities for pupils to develop leadership skills include the Young Interpreters programme. This recognises the huge potential that exists within each school community for pupils of all ages to use their skills and knowledge to support new learners of English so that they feel safe, settled and valued from the start. Young Interpreters undergo specific training to prepare for this role and are selected on the basis of different personal qualities they may have. The support they can offer to a newly arrived pupil can be very reassuring from a parent or carer's point of view at a time when their child may be adapting to substantial changes. The interpreters are also able to support school staff in a variety of ways during the school day.

Building on and knitting together all of these strands of engagement, and others like them that have been nurtured and developed over time, has enabled Goldington to bring stakeholders together into a larger conversation to seek to build a shared understanding around school purpose. Goldington is still exploring how best to do this, but this is how it began.

The chosen starting point for the first stakeholder conversation was a live issue, not a made-up or an imposed one. At the time of writing, the school was just completing the process of becoming a full-age primary school. It was starting to think about how to prepare its first Year 6 children to transition to their chosen secondary schools in a year's time. It decided the place to start was to listen to their pupils. As assistant headteacher Michaela Viola says:

> What we've learned is the actual power of pupil voice and how it can move this school forwards in terms of making a difference. What do children think about their learning? What do they think about the curriculum? How would they make a difference? If they were to teach that lesson, what would they do differently? Actually, getting their point of view and realising that no matter what age they are, a person is still a person and they have their ideas and their thinking.[24]

24. All quotes in this case study are drawn from interviews with one of the authors 30.1.19

By talking about the transition to pupils, staff discovered that the concerns and questions they had were ones that had not actually occurred to staff. As a result, staff and pupils together decided it would be worth examining the experience of other schools that had been through a similar process. A visit was arranged to meet Year 7 pupils in a secondary school in a different local area, who had come from a newly established primary school and so were the first cohort to transition. Goldington pupils prepared questions for the Year 7 staff and pupils, conducted interviews, then came back and analysed the results.

Meanwhile, staff also established a small focus group of parents, drawn from those who were going to be affected by this transition. The parents agreed to meet on two occasions at the start of the school day for a coffee and to share their concerns and questions with members of the senior leadership team. A SurveyMonkey questionnaire was also shared with all parents.

On the back of all this research, Goldington staff were able to allay some concerns and, more importantly, to draw up an action plan for the transition. Another decision that made an important difference was to start to engage another key group of stakeholders: the secondary schools to which the pupils were transferring. This involved taking their input into account, as well as sharing overall conclusions with them so both Goldington and the secondary schools could improve their transitions in the future.

In summary, then, Goldington's joined-up approach to breaking down barriers to engagement started with establishing a sharing culture and a welcoming environment throughout the school. The school's considered deployment of its staff is another crucial ingredient in its success. The commitment to broadening stakeholder engagement is also reflected in the roles of senior leaders, emphasising that this is no add-on luxury. To be successful in this, there must also be close and constant communication across the whole team.

The staffing arrangements have evolved by looking at the skillset of staff and building on that. This has enabled the school to identify and employ a local person as a family worker, and to develop the role of equality and diversity leader within the senior team, spanning school and community.

It has required clear-sighted risk-taking in budgeting at times, but in the words of Caroline Skingsley:

> Start with the human resources and work out how to invest in those first. Be clear what roles you need and want to invest in, and what you want to develop people into.

Developing reciprocity at Fairfield

Lesson six: securing effective and reciprocal engagement involves combining structure and organisation with great flexibility, openness and responsiveness.

Fairfield High School devotes time and energy to establishing a strong sense of community, which includes a shared understanding that with that membership come both rights and responsibilities. The sense of community starts within the school building but importantly also extends beyond it. The care with which pupils are inducted into the community when they join (see chapter 11) is mirrored in the school's commitment to ensure they develop the skills and understanding to engage not just with the school but with the wider global society.

A citizenship programme runs all the way through from Year 7 to Year 11, and all students are required to take a GCSE in Citizenship. This means that every year students will undertake, for example, some work on diversity, rights and responsibilities, values, safeguarding, employability and relationships, as part of a spiral curriculum.

Students are encouraged, both through the programme and through the wider school ethos, to develop as tolerant, independent-minded, interested and curious individuals. They therefore understand political processes, for instance, quite early on, because these are an active part of both a culture and also explicit practice in which they participate.

The school operates a formal student council, as do many schools. Each tutor group elects two representatives to the council. They meet regularly under the oversight of a member of staff who runs the meetings. The student representatives will present their proposals for change to the senior leadership team.

However, this is only the first tier of student leadership. As well as the formal school council, a number of other initiatives for change are encouraged which are more spontaneous and more directly student-led. One example is 'Fairfield Against Apathy'.

This was established by a student in Year 10 a few years ago and has been sustained each year by new students taking on a range of initiatives, both large and small, such as raising money for micro-financing charities. It is described by school leaders as 'an attitude' rather than a formal organisation. The founding student went on to secure a place to study law at Oxford. His experience of establishing and leading such a successful initiative evidently impressed at interview and helped him to secure this highly competitive place.

The school also supports a range of clubs which are about having a social conscience, such as an LGBT club and a feminist society. These are embedded aspects of the school and the students involved in those two clubs in particular have trained staff and other students around those areas. Staff oversee the clubs, but they are student-led. The agenda is student-driven, with only very light-touch supervision. Staff are just there to act as the adult who can supervise and make things happen if needed.

Some things at the school do just happen. A couple of students decided they wanted to save the bees and felt sufficiently empowered to set up a project to do so. They knew exactly who to go to for help to facilitate that and, in the end, they raised several hundred pounds for a charity devoted to keeping bees safe. Assistant vice-principal Farina Ackerman comments:

> Our students do feel that they can raise an issue, and they have a voice and a forum should they wish to do that. It's just about empowering everybody as much as possible and engaging everybody as much as possible.[25]

The creative arts play a strong role in promoting engagement, drawing on close links developed between the head of creative arts and Watershed, a local arts centre. Fairfield's head of creative arts spends time at Watershed working on those links, forming projects with the Watershed

25. All the quotes in this case study are drawn from interviews with one of the authors 5.2.19

staff, as well as organising theatre nights to which parents are invited. These are fully accessible, with interpreters and signers for the deaf. A key focus is to make sure these opportunities are taken by all students, not just the most advantaged, and so take-up is carefully monitored.

Fairfield Parents Network meets independently of the school. While it provides a forum for grievances, more importantly it offers a chance to become involved in the school community, to volunteer time and services, as well as to undertake some fundraising. As Farina says:

> People don't necessarily want to join but they do want to contribute. They don't necessarily have time, and they certainly don't want to speak at meetings, but they would gladly bring some food from their culture. Our job is to look at barriers to engagement and see if we can find ways of making time for people to contribute in a way that works for them.

The school also gathers information about parents' careers and all the skills they can offer so as to create opportunities to bring parents into school to share their skills as aspirational role models for students.

As well as working with parents, Fairfield draws in university PhD students to conduct workshops or after-school clubs with pupils, for instance in music or languages. The aim is for every department to have a relationship with and access to support from local universities.

Perhaps the two most crucial elements of all these relationships is the emphasis on their reciprocal nature, and the way this is developed around a shared focus on nurturing and supporting the learning of pupils. This in turn requires an ethos of trust and respect, along with a systematic encouragement of engagement through removing the barriers which prevent it.

Tools and strategies for encouraging participation and engagement

Our discussion has focused around three key stakeholder groups: parents, students and the wider community. We have stressed throughout the need to develop new models of engagement, based on mutual respect and trust, removing barriers to engagement, and developing shared conversations to better support student learning.

For each of the three groups, we offer just one tool that may be helpful to school leaders approaching that task. These are not intended to be exhaustive, rather just something to start the ball rolling.

1. Parent engagement

For schools seeking to strengthen the engagement of parents with children's learning, the Parental Engagement Toolkit developed by Janet Goodall and colleagues at the University of Bath may be particularly helpful.

The Toolkit is based on research about parents' engagement with children's learning. It does not offer a 'solution'; rather it provides schools with tools to design, enact and evaluate their own processes. The Toolkit is not meant to offer 'one best way' or even best practice in relation to parental engagement, but allows schools to find their own solutions to issues arising in their local contexts.

You can download this for free at: www.bath.ac.uk/publications/parental-engagement-toolkit/attachments/parental-engagement-toolkit.pdf

2. Student engagement

Schools that are interested in developing the ideas of student-led research and Learner Action Teams (see pages 135-6 above) may find the following guidelines (drawn from the work of Roger Holdsworth)[26] useful as a checklist and tool to help shape their thinking.

Step 1: Teacher preparation

This first step involves the development of a shared understanding of what we want to do, including the theory behind the Learner Action Team approach and a commitment to student decision-making on real issues. It also includes planning for how this might fit into the curriculum, identification of possible partners and resources, and setting up the challenges.

This phase is driven by questions to schools and teachers: *What is this about? What are the external expectations? What are our views of students' roles?* Who will be involved? Its objectives are for the development of a shared commitment to the approach, the definition of the broad topic, specification of any external constraints and structures, and identification of funding and management structures.

Step 2: Engagement with the issue

The second step involves the identification of a real problem, challenge or issue: one in which it is not yet known what the outcomes might be, and to which students can bring some 'expertise' to achieve a solution. This challenge is put to the students in a way that can engage their commitment. Here the role of the outsider is important: someone to 'commission' the students, to challenge them to research and act, and to provide an audience for them to report to. Where Learner Action Teams operate within a cluster of schools, this challenge could usefully occur at an inter-school student forum.

This engagement is driven by questions to the students such as: *What is this issue all about? What is the importance of it? To whom? Why? And then crucially: Do we want to do this? Why?*

---

26. You can access *Connect*, Roger's regular electronic magazine about student leadership, at http://research.acer.edu.au/connect.

Step 3: Research

During these school-based steps, the students start by developing definitions of the research questions (what we already know, what we need to find out), and research methods (how we might carry out the research). It is sometimes useful to think about two research steps based on:

- what the issue **is** within our community (e.g. defining or prioritising the issue)
- what the issue is **about** (deeper research into the nature, causes etc. of the issue).

Students then carry out their research. This step is driven by questions to students such as: *What do we know already? What do we need to find out? How will we do this?*

Then, as the research process develops, they ask questions that define their methods: *Who? How? How many? When? What instruments? What questions?*

As they conduct research, they ask: *How is it going? Are we keeping to the timeline? What gaps? What changes should we make to our approach?*

Students will need to develop and implement a structure for data collection, defining their methods, questions, observations and ways of recording this.

Step 4: Reporting the research

Reporting involves telling someone 'external' what has been found out. This might involve giving a report on the research phase to the 'outsider' (the group or person commissioning the research), to other students, or to the community as a whole. In a cluster of schools, this could be the focus of a second student forum.

There are both analysis and communication questions involved here:

- *What did we do? (A summary of the methods.)*
- *What did we find out?*
- *What is it like now? (An overall description.)*
- *What differences exist within the results?*
- *Who do we need to tell?*

Step 5: Designing the action

These 'pre-action' steps are concerned with possible changes that are suggested by the research:

- *What is the big possibility for what could be achieved?*
- *What do we want to change for this to be achieved?*

Initially this involves making decisions on preferred outcomes, then on what needs to be done to achieve those outcomes. Students also need to think at this stage about how they will know whether they have changed anything:

- *What information we will need to collect about the way things are before we start our action?*
- *What information will we need to collect later on?*

This phase initially poses questions to students such as:

- *What surprises us about our research?*
- *What concerns us?*
- *Or makes us angry, annoyed, worried? Why?*
- *Do we all agree on this?*

It then moves on to ask:

- *What should it look like?*
- *What do we want to see happening?*
- *What needs to change to make it like that?*
- *What are the barriers to change?*
- *What is needed to overcome these barriers?*

This might involve 'dreaming' of desired outcomes in a changed world. Only then can students be asked:

- *What can we do to bring about that change?*
- *What forms of action can we take?*

Here they consider the options for education, encouragement, enforcement and engineering. They are challenged about the range of actions possible, so that students and schools don't just think about simply making a poster or, on the other hand, having to build something expensive.

Finally, the actions are defined further:

- *What?*
- *When?*
- *Who?*
- *How?*

The outcome should be an action planner and timeline with clear objectives and achievable steps.

Step 6: Implementing the action

Having planned appropriate action, the students then carry out what they have planned: contacting, writing, producing materials, talking, protesting, lobbying and so on. This involves ongoing reflection to ensure not only that they remain on track, but also that they learn about consequences and limitations as others respond to their actions.

As they do this, students are asked:

- *How is it going?*
- *What do we learn as we do this?*

They are also asked to assess the impact of their actions:

- *What has changed?*
- *Why?*
- *How do we know we have made any difference?*

Reflection time is built in; collection of further data (questionnaires or observations) may be required in order to compare before and after.

Step 7: Reporting the action

This step involves telling someone 'external' to the project – the 'outsider', other students or the community – what was achieved. Questions to prepare for this could include:

- *How do we know what was achieved?*
- *What have been the consequences of what we have done?*

At the start of this stage, students consider:

- *Who do we need to tell?*
- *How?*

They consider internal and external audiences, and effective means of presentation. They are accountable for the challenge they took on at the start.

Step 8: Reflecting on the journey

The Learner Action Team should finally look at what was achieved, how it was achieved and what was learnt along the way. The key questions are:

- *What have we achieved?*
- *Where to now? Why? How?*
- *What did we learn?*
- *How could we improve next time?*

This is also a time for celebration, and for a new commitment (which takes us back to the start of the process again!).

A PDF copy of these guidelines can be downloaded from www.flippingschools.net

3. Community engagement

For schools who are looking to engage their wider stakeholders, this does not necessarily require formal structures or representation. One more informal but still purposeful strategy that may be helpful is the process developed by Schools of Tomorrow for starting conversations with stakeholders about what they want and expect from schools. Once again there is no single 'right' approach; local context really matters.

Finding a focus

There a number of possible ways to find a point of entry for starting a conversation with your stakeholders about the purpose of school and what makes a quality education.

Activities may usefully revolve around examining the purpose of the school in and for its communities, as perceived by its stakeholders. What does a good education look like, in its broadest sense? What is the point of going to school? What do our communities want from their school? But to start with such questions could be off-putting and not lead to a shared understanding of the task in hand. Here are a few alternative approaches, offering three broad entry points that you may want to explore. These are not exclusive and inevitably have a degree of overlap.

Stakeholder group

You might choose to begin by bringing together members of one (or more) of your stakeholder groups. You will need to determine who the stakeholders are for your school: parents, pupils, governors, faith groups, voluntary groups, local business members, etc. It may be that it is best to choose one group for an initial focus. (In that case, you will need to decide at what point and in what way would it be desirable to bring different stakeholder groups together.)

Consider as well whether there is a particular place for school students. How might student leaders be involved in designing, planning and implementing stakeholder conversations?

Possible topics for conversation could include the following:

- Good and not-so-good things: describing the good things (past activities) we should build on and the things to do less of or not at all.
- Designing the characteristics and qualities of the future school: what people see, feel and will work towards.

Place

You might decide to focus on those people in your local communities who have a strong social or economic interest in the area your school serves, to find out what they seek from their local school in terms of preparing their young people to understand and shape their futures. Some of these may be known to you already because of your existing links, but there may also be umbrella groups such as a council of voluntary service, a citizens advice bureau or a local chamber of commerce who could point you in new directions as well.

Inevitably this approach raises the question of boundaries, which will almost certainly overlap with other schools, and how you can approach managing these.

A possible approach might include some of the following ideas:

- Creating a timeline of key events in the school/local community, where participants share their stories linked to what they have written on the timeline. This can lead to the beginnings of participants finding common ground.
- Considering how the past can help to plan for the future of the school.
- Describing the good things that the school/community does that it should build on.
- Describing the things that the school/community does not do so well. What things does it do that it should do less of or not at all?
- Discussing current local trends, possibly taken from the media, to raise awareness of key issues for your local communities.
- Trying to establish the current trends that the school can be proud of having dealt with before exploring those areas where more could be done.

- Establishing what the big future questions are that need to be addressed.
- Activities related to the future school that the group wants to see. This does not have to be something static or purely verbal. It might be a creative activity, constructing visual images of change by, for example, using media such as art, video or drama.

You might in time move on to:

- Agreeing future directions and the strategies required to move towards them.
- Working on common values linked to future directions and prioritising them.
- Developing a draft vision statement for the future school that the group wants.
- Establishing action plans for agreed future directions.

Issue

Another approach could be built around a particular issue that concerns your stakeholders, sitting underneath the umbrella question of how well we prepare young people to understand and shape their futures (for example the future of work, or mental health and wellbeing).

There is a range of possible stimuli that might be useful in initiating this, for instance:

- Films on the chosen issue. These might be documentaries or dramas.
- Speakers from different perspectives and interest groups, local or national.
- PowerPoint presentations.
- Activities, such as World Café or Open Space Technology.[27]

27. See http://www.theworldcafe.com/key-concepts-resources/world-cafe-method/ and https://openspaceworld.org/wp2/what-is/.

Practical issues for consideration include the following:

How will participants be invited?

- How many are you seeking to take part?
- How can you ensure that you are not only reaching the 'usual suspects'?
- What form should the invitation take to make it attractive and readable?
- How far ahead should the invitation be issued to get a good response?

To what will they be invited?

- Is this some special event or is it part of an existing arrangement?
- Consider issues of where, when and for how long. Is school the best venue?
- A school might be an intimidating place for some so does it make more sense to go to where people are, rather than expect them to come to you?
- What is an optimum time and duration? The timing is crucial to attracting the largest and most varied number of stakeholders.
- Is it a one-off at this stage or part of a series of engagements?
- Refreshments?
- What is the hook to persuade people to take the time to be involved?

What will be done with the results?

- How will outcomes be shared? With participants? With others?
- What is the relationship of the emerging stakeholder conversation strategy to the school's governance structures?

A PDF copy of these guidelines can be downloaded from www.flippingschools.net

14. Connected Leadership: A Hub of Networks and Support for Learning

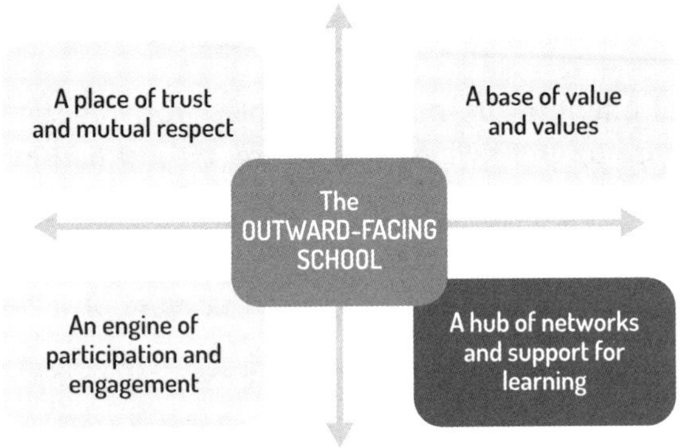

Some principles

The genealogy of leadership, stretching back to Moses, Plato and Confucius, points to a rich and diverse range of usages that have become deeply embedded in the collective unconsciousness of many societies, notably the intertwined concepts of hierarchy, patriarchy and bureaucracy. As great civilisations waxed and waned, so these elements of leadership became deeper and deeper embedded until they acquired a status that makes them axiomatic to most forms of organisation. Leadership in many contexts has become symbiotic with hierarchical status, personal power and control. The dominant social imaginary or consensual view of leadership is reinforced by monotheism and by philosophical models such as Plato's philosopher kings.

The prevailing norms of leadership in human society cling to the historical model of individual ascendancy and the deployment of functions through hierarchy, as occurred in feudal England. Multi-national corporations, military units, churches, schools, operating theatres, rock groups and sports teams all most commonly have hierarchy as their default model. The lack of a leader, or the failure of leadership, is perceived as a dystopian model of society and is used to explain defeat, whether for a sports team or a military unit.

> … in the vastly different circumstances of today – different because of the radical changes that culture has imposed on modern life and the environments we live in – we respond as though we were still on the plains of Africa, hunting wild game and spearing our enemies from over the hill. We respond by instinct rather than judgement. (Dunbar 2010, p.161)

When linked with hierarchical power, the instinctual approach explains much of the inappropriate behaviour found in corporate life and politics. This is how power corrupts, but this negative model is not inevitable. Another understanding of leadership is emerging, summarised in Table 6.

Comparing the behaviours that exemplify the potential of an alternative approach to leadership allows for a comparison between traditional and emerging models of leadership. The historical model will undoubtedly continue in some contexts, for example certain uniformed services, but even in that context there is the potential for change and the introduction of different perspectives on what constitutes effective leadership.

Historical model	Emerging model
Power resides in one person	Authority is shared
Autonomous decision-making	Evidence-based decisions
Hierarchy	Flatarchy
Works through control	Works through trust
Top-down accountability	Mutual accountability
Individual status	Collective capacity

Table 6: Changing Patterns of Leadership

The Orpheus Chamber Orchestra was formed in 1972 and is famous for the fact that it is a world-class ensemble that performs without a conductor. The orchestra currently has 27 members, and performs a mixture of classical repertoire and new compositions. Even though it is smaller than many orchestras, its repertoire is complex and challenging. It is often described as a leaderless orchestra but that is to miss the crucial point:

> Precisely because there is no conductor each player must help decide about musical interpretations. Each one must take part of the responsibility for ensuring that musical entrances are together, that themes are passed smoothly from section to section, and that the composer's vision for a piece is realized beautifully and musically. (Seifter 2001, p.xi)

In other words, it offers us an alternative perspective on leadership and how it can be exercised, which challenges many of those historical assumptions and norms.

Seifter argues that the factors which allow the orchestra to work consistently at a very high level of performance include:

- Giving workers control of their work.
- Encouraging personal responsibility for the quality of the work.
- Defining roles and relationships.

- Sharing and rotating leadership.
- Distributing leadership with cross-structural teams.
- Working through dialogue.
- Building consensus through creative structures.
- Securing passionate commitment to vision and mission.

Orpheus effectively works as a community. Each of the factors listed above are significant in their own right, but taken together, working through mutual reinforcement and interdependence, they have the potential to create a powerful nexus, strongly redolent of high social capital in the way they all share a focus on human interaction and relationships.

There are obviously issues of scale in terms of the potential to follow the Orpheus model. Would it work with an orchestra of 60 to 80 performing a Bruckner or Mahler symphony? Possibly not, but that still does not justify the hero conductor, the 'maestro', working through fear and compliance, supported by a giant ego and by our willingness to defer to alleged charisma. It rather raises the possibility that large, unwieldy groups should be broken up into their constituent elements to work separately before being brought together. And indeed, this is what actually happens in practice with the Orpheus Orchestra. Leadership is distributed according to need and effectiveness; it is deployed according to skills and ability rather than status.

Seifter's eight factors can be synthesised into three key themes that help to inform leadership in the context of building networks and developing community. The three themes relate to the moral basis for the community, the significance of networks and relationships, and rethinking the role of the school as a hub for networks working interdependently. We will look at each of these in turn.

Morally informed, consensual practice

Values are axiomatic to schools as organisations and, equally, the leadership of education has to be seen as a moral act. It is very difficult to find any examples of decision-making in education that does not have moral implications. The relationships with stakeholders are therefore, of necessity, rooted in shared values.

> The heart of the school as a moral community is its covenant of shared values. This covenant provides the basis for determining its morality ... the virtuous school subscribes to and uses these moralities as a basis for deciding what its values are and how they will be pursued. (Sergiovanni 1992, p.108)

One of the defining characteristics of successful communities is that they have a high degree of moral consensus or alignment on key issues. This is manifested in what is sometimes described as consensual authoritarianism. This phrase describes situations where there is a high degree of agreement about the basis on which a community should function. Such a consensus derives its authority from consistent application of what might be best described as a social contract rooted in fundamental values.

Values are the cement or glue of community building; they are the means by which all the disparate elements are linked and united and become mutually reinforcing. The key means of creating social capital are dialogue and storytelling to illuminate and exemplify the processes of building a collective sense of identity that is at the heart of authentic community development.

There seems little doubt that the development of a moral community is one of the key leadership roles in any context. The development of a moral consensus, securing engagement and compliance with that consensus, and ensuring that there is a high degree of interaction between principle and practice, are all higher-order leadership imperatives.

In most contexts it would seem that leadership language and behaviour are the pivotal factors. Communities with high social capital are led by people who 'walk the talk' and 'do the right thing'. These phrases are clichés, but they are clichés because they are true. Leaders use and enact the moral language of the community.

If schools are to function as democratic learning communities then there has to be parity of esteem across the community so that everyone is treated with the same level of dignity and respect in exactly the same way that we expect fairness and consistency in the health centre, the garage and the restaurant. Children and young people are very sensitive to these issues and aware of what they regard as a lack of fairness. It is important they have opportunities to explore the moral vocabulary of the community and understand how it works in practice. Thinking about values has wider implications than talking through challenging issues:

> ... there's good evidence that children, even fairly young children, can think philosophically. And, while more research needs to be done, there is a growing body of evidence that it is good for them academically, socially and emotionally. The kind of skills such philosophy programmes foster are surely just the sort of skills we need new citizens to develop. (Law 2006, p.39)

Teaching thinking, in its various manifestations, is clearly a powerful source of cultural capital, while also making a significant contribution to social capital. Open, analytical discussion is one of the best ways of building consensus and developing the framework for renewing the community through shared learning. So it is important that pupils are able to set the agenda, with plenty of opportunities to discuss the issues that they face as they mature, such as:

- The climate change crisis.
- Ethnicity.
- Social networks and relationships, and the place of social media.
- LGBT rights and identity.
- Diet, including veganism and vegetarianism.
- Refugees and immigrants.
- The ageing population and dementia.

These are all issues that are real now. Most will increasingly influence the lives of the current school cohort. It would be naïve to pretend that consensus is easy to achieve on such issues, but this is all the more reason to devote more time in trying to build it.

As well as securing equity as a norm for all, to work towards moral leadership in the community requires leaders to model appropriate behaviours in such a way as to concretely exemplify the key principles. A classic example of this strategy in practice is the issue of respect and dignity for all members of the community. The ways in which these elements of community life might be modelled is through something as simple and basic as courtesy. In many ways, courtesy is the tangible expression of empathy, awareness, recognition and kindness.

It is not enough for leaders to develop a coherent and valid set of moral precepts; they have to be understood, accepted and then acted on by the leader, so they become the norm in how that leader is perceived. In his book *The Tipping Point*, Malcolm Gladwell (2000) tells the story of Paul Revere's ride to warn communities across New England that 'the British are coming!'. At the same time that Revere rode north, William Dawes rode south. But Dawes failed to make any contact with local leaders, whereas on the northern route the local militias were immediately mobilised. Revere was what Gladwell calls a connector. He was gregarious and intensely social:

> He was a fisherman and a hunter, a card player and a theatre-lover, a frequenter of pubs and a successful businessman. He was active in the local masonic lodge and a member of several social clubs. (Gladwell 2000, p.58)

Connectors are human hubs; they relate to and engage with rich and complex networks. They like people and are very good at remembering names, relatives and birthdays. They also spread good news and facilitate meetings and interactions. It would be possible, but very complicated, to draw a sociogram of Revere's various networks and the way his different types of contacts overlap and interact. Revere might well be a good model for the leadership of the outward-facing school (although we are not advocating emulating his full range of different types of relationships – far too exhausting!).

Revere was successful because of his focus on people, but by itself that was not enough. He was also, in Gladwell's terms, a maven. He gathered ideas and information and, crucially, shared them. He thus contributed to the collective intelligence of the community, ensuring that it was able to respond to changes in appropriate and effective ways. In many ways, Revere provides us with a model of what we increasingly understand to be effective through the study of social networks. His ride was very much the 'right thing' and his actions led to the desired outcome. In other words, he made an impact.

One of the key leadership challenges in education is the extent to which there is a clear, causal relationship between intention and impact. MacAskill (2015) and Singer (2015) have raised a number of concerns about charitable giving, exploring the implications of what Singer refers to as 'effective altruism' and MacAskill as 'doing good better'. Their central concern is whether in giving to a charity we are actually making a difference. Is our donation leading to an impact on an area of need? How might we prioritise our giving? How do we decide if it is better to give to Guide Dogs UK or to support Sightsavers in their work to prevent river blindness, balancing remediation, cure and prevention? Education and medicine are full of such dilemmas that leaders have to engage with and resolve.

In the traditional model of hierarchical decision-making, one person, or a small cabal, would take decisions based on their personal interests, their value system and their anecdotal experience. This led to the following situation in medicine:

> … just a few decades ago, best medical practice was driven by things like eminence, charisma, and personal experience. We needed the help of statisticians, epidemiologists, information librarians, and experts in trial design to move forwards. Many doctors – especially the most senior ones – fought hard against this, regarding 'evidence-based medicine' as a challenge to their authority. (Goldacre 2013, p.4)

Evidence-based decision-making is usually associated with what might be described as academic practice, with concern for validity and reliability, epistemological integrity and methodological consistency. Sometimes, randomised controlled trials are perceived as the 'gold standard' for this. However, in reality the picture is a much more subtle. Indeed, it could be that while randomised trials probably have the greatest integrity in terms of evidence, the very nature of their process inhibits understanding the full potential of a topic to be investigated.

Sackett et al. provide a much more nuanced interpretation of evidence-based medicine:

> Evidence-based medicine is the conscientious, explicit, and judicious use of current best evidence in making decisions about the care of individual patients. The practice of evidence-based medicine means integrating individual clinical expertise with the best available external clinical evidence from systematic research. By individual clinical expertise we mean the proficiency and judgment that individual clinicians acquire through clinical experience and clinical practice. (Sackett et al. 1996, p.71)

Building on this understanding, it might therefore be more appropriate to talk of evidence-informed practice in education. This demonstrates the same respect for academic research but, as in medicine, also acknowledges the contribution of professional practice and personal experience, the need for interpretation, and the relevance of context. It recognises, too, the deep necessity for professionals to continue to learn, to understand the nature of evidence, to keep knowledge up-to-date, to question, challenge, and pay very close attention to impact.

There are a number of reasons why evidence-based/informed practice is being seen as a better way of working in schools. Firstly, it means that teachers and school leaders are increasingly in control of key decisions, as they have the evidence to guide what are often complex decision-making processes. Secondly, evidence-informed approaches, combined with school-based research, means that teachers are able to focus their professional learning on actual practice in the classroom. Thirdly, in times of economic stringency, evidence-informed approaches can help to ensure that scarce resources are used to best effect and make the greatest impact on teaching and learning.

In summary, connected moral leadership is data-driven, drawing on a wide range of evidence and working through networks to secure engagement in high-quality decision-making based on objectivity and professional understanding. The most effective community is likely to be research-informed, with much of that learning involving networked communities of practice.

Networks and relationships

It is impossible to say which comes first in the development of social capital: consensus around values or effective relationships. As is so often the case, the truth probably falls somewhere between the two. The two elements are involved in an interactive, iterative process that means constant review, reflexivity and innovation. For Fritjof Capra, networks work through autopoiesis, i.e. self-renewal:

> For an organisation to be alive ... the existence of social networks is not sufficient; they have to be networks of a special type. Living networks ... are self-generating ... In this way the entire network generates itself producing a common context of meaning, shared knowledge, rules of conduct a boundary and a collective identity. (Capra 2002, p.94)

The importance of networking has long been reflected in its supportive technology; the Rolodesk business-card holder was superseded by the Filofax filing system, which in turn was replaced by the mobile phone contacts list. The number of contacts, in whatever technology, was taken as a sign of success and influence. The move from mechanical to virtual storage and retrieval provides a powerful metaphor for significant aspects of social and organisational change. The ability to network has become one of the defining skills and behaviours necessary to develop cultural and social capital. What might be called the technology of networking provides a useful quantitative and qualitative measure of cultural and social capital.

It is very important to distinguish between developing networks and social networking using information technology. The full significance and potential of the latter are yet to be fully explored. While there are many positives associated with platforms such as Facebook, LinkedIn and Twitter, there are also some fundamental issues around ownership and confidentiality that need to be resolved at an international level. Social media might be seen as consisting of essentially immature networks; they lack a real consensus about what is and is not appropriate to communicate. Equally, there is minimal accountability for abusing a network.

Living and working in a community requires sophisticated social interaction in order to maximise social and cultural capital. Putnam makes a pivotal link between social capital, community and networks, and hence the relationships expressed through networks and norms.

> ... the presence of social capital – individuals connected to one another through trusting networks and common values – allows for the enforcement of common standards ... Social networks may also provide emotional and financial support. (Putnam 2000, p.312)

The formal induction process common to many organisations, and to communities in equally significant but often more intangible ways, is a classic example of securing social capital and so reinforcing the sense of community. Thus, the Sunday morning football team, the scout troop, and numerous other groups share the central significance of engaging with the relevant norms and securing access to appropriate networks. There would appear to be a very high correlation between building social capital and investing in norms and networks. For Pentland, norms and networks are interdependent with the expression and development of positive relationships.

> We are traders in ideas, goods, favours and information and not simply the competitors that traditional market thinking would make us. In each area of our lives we develop a network of trusted relationships and favour those ties over others. Exchanges within this network of trusted social ties facilitate idea flow, creating an inclusive, vigorous culture and are responsible for the collective intelligence of our society. (Pentland 2014, p.130)

Using a range of sources, Christakis and Fowler (2011) identify a number of propositions about the nature and functioning of social networks:[28]

28. 'The networks we create have lives of their own. They grow, change, reproduce, survive and die. Things flow and move within them. A social network is like a superorganism, with an anatomy and a physiology – a structure and function – of its own. From bucket brigades to blogospheres, the human superorganism does what no person could do on their own.' (Christakis and Fowler 2011, p.289)

- Humans make and remake their networks all the time in terms of both membership and structure. They are dynamic and change to reflect changes in the environment in which they function.
- Just as individuals influence the network, so the network changes people. The dynamics of social interactions are reflected in changes in status, significant relationships and wellbeing.
- We are influenced by those closest to us (family and friends) as well as by those who are more remote (friends of friends, people working in other departments, etc.).
- Social networks are dynamic; they can behave in ways that are not controlled or initiated by one person. A helpful analogy is seen in starlings flocking; in a murmuration, several thousand birds fly in harmony without any apparent overall coordination. It seems that the birds fly in relationship with their immediate neighbours.
- Some individuals are disproportionately influential in how a network functions (Paul Revere is one example, as discussed previously in this chapter) because they have more sophisticated relationships, greater access to intelligence and more effective positive social interactions.
- Networks can grow and extend, sub-divide, change their original purpose and die. The loss of a significant member can lead to a fundamental reorientation.

At this point, it is important to stress that networks and relationships are not only socially important; they play a very significant role in our psychological and emotional wellbeing. Living and working in a culture of high trust and openness, with a range of relationships of different degrees of engagement and commitment, is very good for individuals and the wider community, as Dunbar (2010) demonstrates in his highly significant study. The answer to that question, incidentally, would appear to be a maximum of 150 people of varying degrees of significance. We return to this in chapter 17.

Networks need to work at a number of levels – essentially from the neural to the global – to be successful and effective. Networks determine mental health, organisational effectiveness, a strong economy, international relations and world peace. Failure usually occurs at any level because the relevant network is not functioning appropriately or effectively. This applies equally to the classroom, the school and the community it serves. Dysfunctional individual and group behaviour is often a manifestation of a failure of networking.

Schools obviously have a range of networks. In secondary schools, subject departments may well function as closed networks, having minimal engagement with the rest of the school. One of the challenges of the academy movement in England is the functioning of multi-academy trusts (MATs). As a MAT grows, from a few schools to perhaps up to 15 schools, so the networks have to change. Factors such as geographical proximity, historical partnerships, Ofsted status, and the personal relationships of school leaders will all serve to complicate the nature of working relationships. While networks will often be complex in their own right, they are also one of the most effective ways of managing the complexity of relationships, both in and between schools.

The role of the school as a hub

The concept of the hub is central to many aspects of cultural and social capital. It is a practical expression of intervention strategies to promote community engagement. In essence, a hub is a nodal point where many routes meet or intersect, such as the transport hub in a local town that brings together the railway station, bus station and car parking on to one site. In another example, a local village hall might act as a hub by providing a post office, pharmacy and library, as well as catering facilities and the equipment for drama and musical events.

In many villages and urban communities, the school is the most significant public resource available to the community, and yet it is closed for 12 weeks a year and not open after 5pm or at weekends. However, the potential for school engagement in many communities (as embodied, for example, in the extended school concept) has been seriously compromised by a range of factors:

> Schools feel they are restricted in what they can provide because of limited funding, despite an apparent unanimous desire to expand extended services further and positive assessments on their outcomes. Provision is orientated largely towards pupils rather than the wider community, but older children are less engaged. There is also an unmet demand for both term-time and holiday childcare within schools. Crucially, our evidence exposes a divide in interest towards after-school activities between more advantaged and disadvantaged groups, despite evidence suggesting that the latter could benefit most from extended services. (Diss and Jarvie 2016, p.46)

If the implications are carefully thought through, at both local and governmental level, extended or full-service schools would seem to offer a potential response to many of the issues highlighted in previous chapters, given their potential to enhance wellbeing and engagement, and so contribute towards academic success as well as raising cultural capital.

Social entrepreneurship

The potential for developing any community is largely contingent on the extent to which it develops social capital, and that in turn depends upon social entrepreneurship. Just as economic capital for business depends on economic entrepreneurship (for example raising funds), so communities require the growth of social capital if they are to flourish.

Following the publication of his seminal work *Bowling Alone* in 2000, Robert Putnam reports that he was sent numerous examples of successful community initiatives. He published a range of these in *Better Together* and wrote a detailed analysis of the criteria for successful community projects. They are:

- Careful analysis of the 'structural conditions': those factors which are available to support an initiative, such as accessible resources and existing policies and strategies.
- The use of 'federation': nesting smaller groups within larger groups to enhance a sense of belonging and commitment, and to foster personal relationships.

- Fostering social ties and interdependence by developing an overarching and shared sense of belonging through common purpose and shared values.
- Recognising the need for ownership through the development and respect for people's own stories, building the capacity for dialogue.
- Building multi-stranded networks of shared interest and common concern which utilize a wide range of communication technologies.

In many communities, schools are the most significant resource, hence the significance of the village primary school as a key element in the development of necessary levels of social capital. For example, on 7 May 2019, the BBC News website ran a feature on North Denes Primary School in Great Yarmouth, describing it as 'the fourth emergency service' (Clahane and Shields 2019).

According to the feature, following a visit to a pupil's home, headteacher Debbie Whiting was shocked to discover a level of food poverty of which she had been completely unaware. Dismayed at what she found, Whiting went shopping for the family. But she realised that, if one family was struggling in silence, there were likely to be others. So, she discussed with staff the idea of starting a food collection.

The food bank began slowly, filled at first with donations from teachers and parents, supplemented by funding raised from community groups. About half a dozen families a week use the service. Parents can request an emergency package to see a family of four through a week's worth of meals. Those who feel embarrassed are able to pick up their supplies from a side door, out of sight from other parents.

Debbie Whiting says that 'When people have got nowhere else to turn, they turn to us. We've uncovered more and more need. The more you ask, the more you find out – there's a level of hidden poverty that you would not be aware of.'

Yet the problems of poverty cannot be solved simply by food parcels. One third of children arriving in reception class at North Denes are classed as obese and, by the time they get to Year 6, this has risen to half. The school has responded by starting to run six-week courses teaching parents how to cook nutritious food on a budget.

The staff at North Denes know they do not have to provide the extra support they give. They also know the impact if they do not. Children who are not fed, warm or safe do not learn well, and can behave badly or miss school. 'All these things, they are all part of enabling children to be in a place where they can learn', says Debbie Whiting.

The Audit Commission, in their 2006 report *More Than The Sum*, provided some very clear and practical guidelines for any school seeking to engage with its wider community. They suggest:

- Working in partnership with local public services, the community and other schools is integrated into the vision, management plans and day-to-day working of the school.
- Support for families is seen as central to better educational outcomes.
- The concept of community goes wider than children and parents.
- The school is seen as a community resource by staff, pupils, governors and local people.
- Community engagement is promoted as important for all staff.
- There are high expectations and aspirations for pupils and the local community alike.
- The school is responsive to community concerns.

Our two lessons from practice that follow show how leaders can help to make this happen, even in times of constrained resources.

Lessons from practice

Making change at Spinney

Lesson seven: successful leadership in a complex environment, such as a school, involves nurturing an environment for changemakers to emerge.

The Spinney is an Ashoka Changemaker school, one of 15 in the UK. This was a conscious choice for the school to pursue and it means the school actively seeks to 'enable all students to become changemakers – young people who have the skills and confidence to change the world for the good of all'.

Change is thus something that involves everyone, at every level in the organisation. But, importantly, it is also primarily outward-facing, not inward-looking, as headteacher Rae Snape makes clear:

> We encourage our pupils to be confident and articulate communicators, to think of themselves as global citizens with a developing awareness of broad social and ecological issues and to understand that they can be changemakers with the power to make a positive difference in their school, community and world. Where appropriate our curriculum links to the United Nations' Sustainable Development Goals.[29]

This means, for example, that pupils are supported to take action within the school in response to climate change, as well as contributing to wider movements for change.

Rae believes her role is primarily to be an enabler. That does not mean enabling a free-for-all. Rather it means establishing and sustaining autonomy, competence and relatedness:

> I want colleagues to be competent to teach well, confident in their own agency, and willing to innovate. My role is to make the last two possible for good teachers, and through them to see that this competence, confidence and willingness to innovate is transmitted to the children. This way there is no disconnect between what we say and what we do at every level. As a changemaker school we manifest in ourselves the values of empathy, creativity, teamwork, leadership

29. One of the targets for the Quality Education goal is: 'By 2030, to ensure that all learners acquire the knowledge and skills needed to promote sustainable development, including, among others, through education for sustainable development and sustainable lifestyles, human rights, gender equality, promotion of a culture of peace and non-violence, global citizenship and appreciation of cultural diversity and of culture's contribution to sustainable development.' (United Nations, no date)

and change-making in the hope that this will transfer to and be evident in the children.

The emphasis in this on each person having agency as a changemaker is striking, as is the role of the leader in making that happen. One of the most important parts of the leader's role concerns story-telling, setting the narrative for the journey in a way which each person can relate to and which reinforces the direction of travel. That is why The Spinney has a team room, not a staff room, and why this is a place for telling celebratory stories, not consuming negative energy complaining about misbehaving children. That is why each Monday begins with a team briefing with three elements: checking in on everyone's emotional wellbeing, a look at the week ahead, and an appreciative reflection by the headteacher, which serves to remind and articulate the common expectations around the shared narrative.

The aim is to recognise and celebrate the uniqueness and preciousness of each individual, and this extends out to include each child. Rae wants to equip staff to feel confident to do the right thing for each child in each moment without reference to dogmatic rules. That is part of what it means to have a culture in which everyone wants to and can contribute, in which everyone is a co-creator and changemaker.

Rae describes herself as an 'educational entrepreneur', someone who likes to invent projects and is always looking to connect ideas and people and to put the pieces of the jigsaw together. And this is not confined to the school, but necessarily involves interaction with the world beyond the school gate, if pupils are truly to develop as she would wish with choices, relationships and agency.

For example, in an interesting recurrence of the theme of creativity which is common to all four schools we have explored, she has been instrumental in helping to initiate My Cambridge. This is a city-wide, cultural education partnership of individuals and organisations committed to ensuring every young person in Cambridge is able to confidently construct their own cultural life, drawing on and feeling connected to the whole of the city in which they live. She also co-designed the Cambridgeshire Festival of Education, an annual event in partnership with the Faculty of Education at Cambridge University, which is a celebration of teachers and teaching. The festival motif is a 'flamingo of hope'.

One vital component in nurturing others to lead requires overcoming personal or organisational ego so as to listen, trust and share leadership. This involves self-awareness and openness, not only for change externally but for change internally as well. As Thai Nguyen (2014) puts it: 'Effective leadership flows from effectively leading yourself. Becoming the best version of yourself will equip you to spark change in others.'

Building a Schools Trust at Homewood

Lesson eight: connected leadership involves perseverance as well as patience, attention to details as well as vision, humility as well as conviction.

The formation of the I-College at Homewood began gradually and carefully, as we saw in chapter 14, but it was also the result of several years of prior ground-laying and preparation, combined with a school leadership holding a clear and coherent purpose, and a sustained attempt to involve all stakeholders in understanding and sharing that purpose.

There was a three-year lead-in to the opening of the I-College, involving research and investigation, discussion and hard thinking. For headteacher Sally Lees, it was crucial this new initiative formed part of an overarching vision and made sense in that context. It was not to be a project or just bolted on to existing provision. Both governors and parents, as well as staff and students, were involved in developing thinking at every stage.

The vision was to put learning at the centre of the college structure and to do that in a way which, in a very large school, gave members some sense of belonging but also contributed to creating a wide range of individual learning pathways.

From this vision, as well as through a long history of working with local primary schools (in ways that extended collaborative working far beyond transition planning), the vision of establishing a Schools Trust for the whole town emerged against the context of ongoing structural reform in the English education system.

Tenterden was of a suitable size and identity for heads to seriously consider a 0–19 learning journey which placed curriculum coherence at its core. This idea included a focus on independent learning, building on the I-Learning programme which had begun to extend out of the I-College into pieces of work with local primary schools. Heads recognised that while independent learners were clearly very much in evidence within early-years settings, the same children by the age of 11 seemed to have lost much of that capability.

In grasping the opportunity provided by this notion, Sally saw it as crucially important to work organically and to build on existing work and relationships. There were a range of strong school and community links already in place and she saw that these might be further strengthened through such a development. They included an annual community arts festival led by the schools with local groups, and involvement with local history and the Tenterden steam railway. What all these community links shared in common was their strong curriculum base. These were not afterthoughts but an important way of making learning real and connected to the world.

But the journey towards Tenterden Schools Trust being established was nevertheless still a long and hard one. Sally was absolutely determined that every school had to be part of the trust or the trust could not happen. Its purpose would have been lost. This made things very complicated, as the primary schools comprised a mix of church schools and other schools, and the diocese was keen to promote a diocese-wide trust.

The negotiation was long and at times difficult, sometimes requiring huge amounts of patience and perseverance to overcome seemingly insuperable obstacles. It meant not giving up and not walking away. It required clarity and steadiness of purpose, but also the capacity to build and nurture trust, and to acquire over time a track record for integrity, conviction and commitment to the common good.

This is a prime example of the sort of 'boundary-spanning leadership' described by Lasker et al. (2001), which is able to 'understand and appreciate partners' different perspectives, bridge their diverse cultures, and be comfortable sharing ideas, resources, and power' (p.193). Such a leader needs acute emotional intelligence, combined with a thick skin and genuine humility. This is no place for rigid hierarchies or 'hero' leaders.

The trust finally came into being with all town-based primary schools on board in September 2016, and it has a number of important features that are worth reflection. It was conceived as a partnership of equals, with each school having equal status, whatever their size. Little things were worked on to secure this; details such as making logos the same size and not having a common uniform were really important statements in practice. The trust took pains to protect the status, role and identity of local governing bodies through very careful and detailed schemes of delegation.

The governing body of Homewood displayed courage and vision in making time available for their headteacher to undertake the partnership-building activity this development required. They recognised both the long-term benefit it could bring to the school as well as the wider benefit to the local community. But it all rested on making sure that the right people were in place in the school leadership to ensure its continued day-to-day success while the wider endeavour was taking shape.

Sally Lees became CEO of the trust, initially combining this with school headship, before giving up the headship and becoming half-time CEO of the trust. Her remit and intention is to grow the trust to include all interested primary schools in the surrounding villages, so as to secure the financial viability of the trust but also to complete its community vision for all children and young people aged 0–19.

Tools and strategies for establishing networks and learning support

1. Network mapping

Every school has a huge range of networks, by virtue of just being there. But that does not mean they are the only networks possible or even the best ones. It can be useful from time to time to take stock and try to map all the networks that you have to identify possible gaps, changes that have occurred, and where more or less effort may now need to be made.

Figure 11 shows the beginning of a partnership map that might be produced by a typical, albeit fictional, secondary school that wished to carry out such an exercise, while Figure 12 shows how these might be expressed in terms of networks and linkages. You can find a blank completely editable version of each to use for your own school mapping to plot your current partnerships and networks, and thus identify areas for development, online at www.flippingschools.net. If you want to further develop your understanding of the complex inter-relationship of these and their impact on your pupils, you may wish in drawing your own version of Figure 12 to vary the size of boxes and lines to reflect your understanding of the relative strength of those relationships at present. .

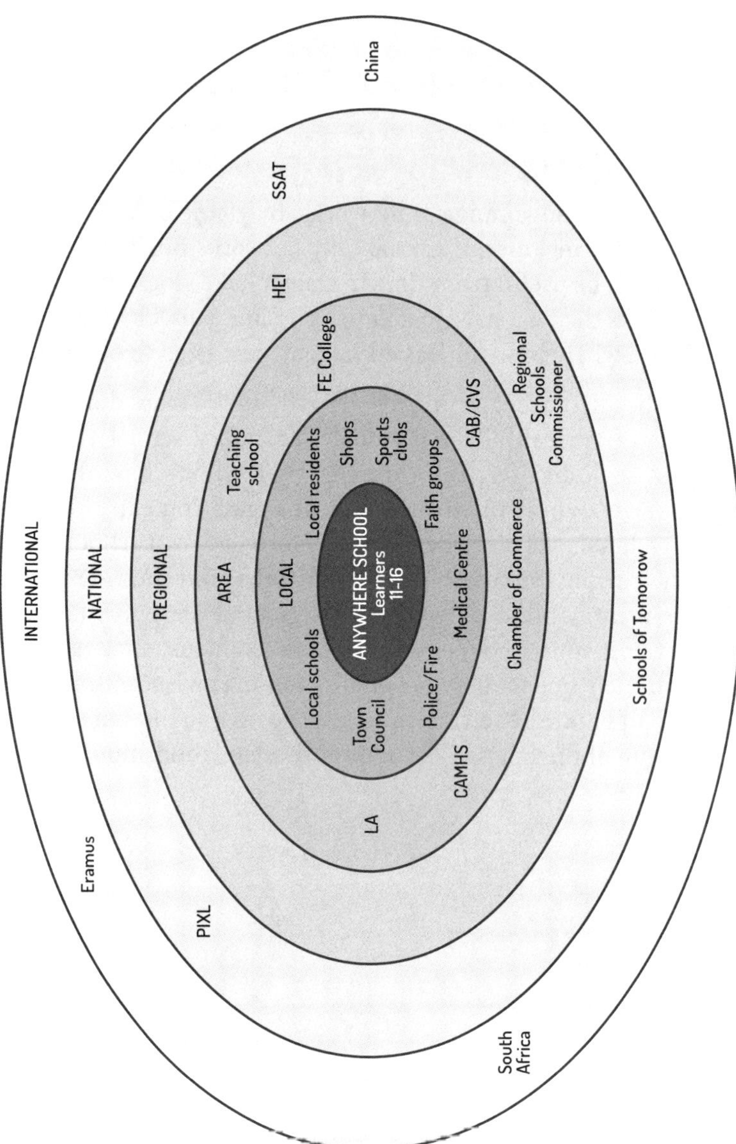

Figure 11: An Example Partnership Map for a Typical Secondary School

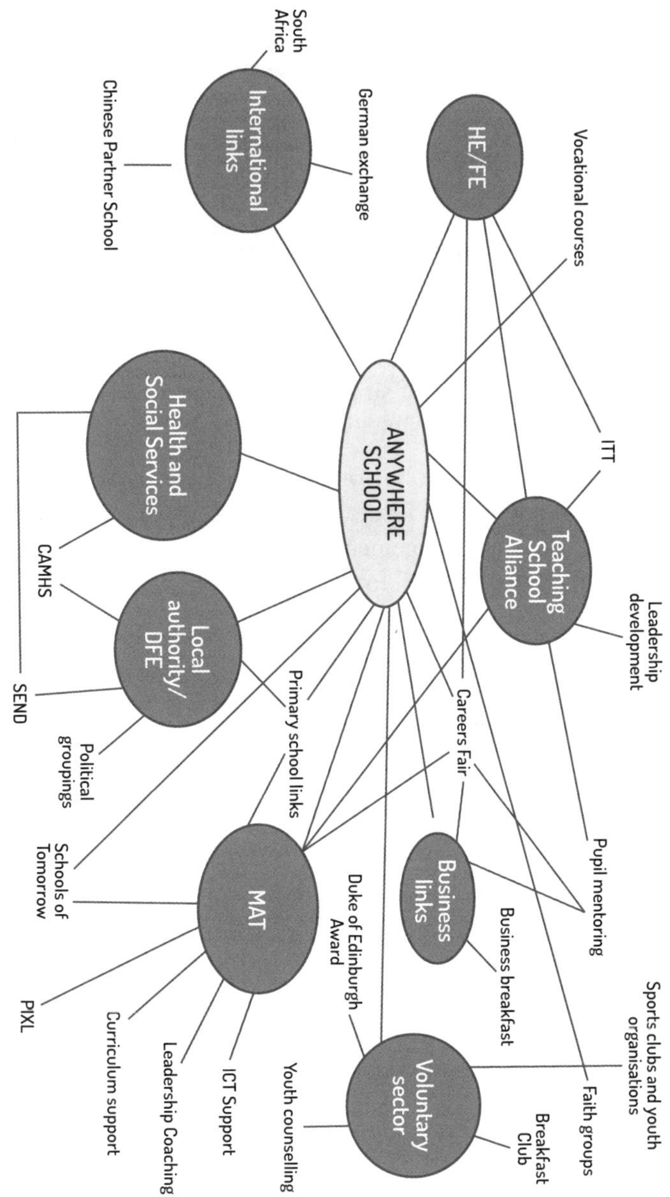

Figure 12: Some of the Ways Those Partnerships Found Expression

2. Where are you now?

We think any school needs to be making use of the four building blocks, introduced and explored in the preceding chapters, if it wants to become an educational builder of social capital. It therefore needs to understand where it is coming from, how others see it, and how effectively it is using the building blocks at present.

As we have stressed throughout, none of the building blocks is simple in itself, and each has a complex inter-relationship with the other three. Moreover, the judgement a leader exercises in determining their starting point and pace of change cannot be a wholly rational or scientific one. It will be influenced by a raft of situational and personal factors, making use of evidence wherever possible (while also recognising its limitations).

To help in that process, we offer one final tool we have developed over several years that any school leader may choose to adapt and use to help inform or confirm their judgements about the quality of relationships and agency within their school (or schools).

This tool utilises a series of separate but linked questionnaires, one for each of three key stakeholder groups (staff, students and parents). As shown in the templates below, a common pattern is followed with mirror questions to which each stakeholder group can respond separately. Each set of questions focuses on perceptions of the school in some key aspects of one of the building blocks. Schools may also wish to add additional questions of their own to any section, but take care to ensure clarity and consistency.

The questions used draw on the UK Social Capital Framework (Harper and Kelly 2003), originally developed by the Office for National Statistics and adapted by the authors for a school setting. The questions also use of elements of Goddard's Social Capital Scale from the USA, adapted in terms of language to English schools. The questionnaires therefore do not purport in any way to form a standardised test, but they do have elements within them that have been subject to wider testing.

Each questionnaire is intended to be used with a five-point Likert scale, indicating strength of agreement or disagreement (1 = strongly disagree, 2 = disagree, 3 = neither agree nor disagree, 4 = agree, 5 = strongly agree).

For each question, the ratings received from each respondent can be aggregated to give an overall average.

A downloadable Word version of the three sets of questionnaires can be accessed online at www.flippingschools.net. Some schools may wish to use these as paper questionnaires, one for staff, for students, and for parents, having smartened up their presentation with logos and other information specific to the school, taking care to make them look and sound as user-friendly as possible. But other schools may choose to import the questions into an online system, such as through SurveyMonkey, which could enable easier analysis of the results.

Two critically important forms of analysis would be to examine any significant differences of perception between stakeholder groups, and to look at trends over time in terms of relative strengths and weaknesses, and how these compare with leaders' own perceptions.

The exercise should be repeated at regular intervals (perhaps yearly) to enable the school to benchmark results and target areas for improvement.

SUMMARY OF STAKEHOLDER PERCEPTION SURVEY QUESTIONS FOR EACH BUILDING BLOCK

A PLACE OF TRUST AND MUTUAL RESPECT		
STUDENTS	**PARENTS**	**STAFF**
The school is an honest place	The school is an honest place	There is a culture of openness and transparency within the school
I feel safe in this school	The school keeps my child safe	I feel safe in this school
Students here are caring towards each other	Students here are caring towards each other	Students here are caring towards each other
I know what the school expects of me	I know what the school expects from me	I know what the school expects from me
My parents trust this school to do what's best	Staff in this school trust the parents	Staff in this school trust the parents
Staff in this school trust the students	Staff in this school trust the students	Staff in this school trust the students
Students in this school trust the staff	I have confidence in the staff of the school	Students in this school trust the staff
Students in this school can be counted on to work hard	My child is expected to work hard at school	Students in this school can be counted on to work hard

THE SCHOOL AND ITS VALUE		
STUDENTS	**PARENTS**	**STAFF**
This school has good facilities	This school has good facilities	This school has good facilities
Its facilities are well used by students and the community	Its facilities are well used by students and the community	Its facilities are well used by students and the community
This school is a good place for me to learn in	The school is a good place for my child to learn in	The school is a good place to work in
I feel that I'm making good progress at school	My child is making good progress at this school	I am encouraged to learn and develop myself
The school is valued by people outside as an important part of the community	The school is seen as an important part of this community	The school is seen as an important part of this community
I am proud to belong to this school	I am proud to be associated with this school	I am proud to be associated with this school

PARTICIPATION AND ENGAGEMENT		
STUDENTS	**PARENTS**	**STAFF**
There is good communication in the school	I am kept well informed about my child's progress	There is good communication in the school
The school listens to me	The school helps me to support my child's learning	Ideas and suggestions are listened to and put into action
I get feedback on my ideas	The school takes account of my suggestions and concerns	I always receive feedback on ideas and suggestions I have made
I feel I can have responsibility for what happens in school	I am able to support the work of the school	I feel I have responsibility for what happens in school
I know the impact I have on the school	I am able to have influence on how the school goes forward	When I see something wrong, I know I can do something about it
I know who the leaders of the school (including students) are	I'm aware of who the school's leaders are	I'm aware of who the school's leaders are and their roles
I know what the school wants to do in the future	I am confident about the direction the school is being led in	I am confident about the direction the school is being led in

SOCIAL NETWORKS AND SUPPORT FOR LEARNING		
STUDENTS	**PARENTS**	**STAFF**
The staff here want me to do well	The staff here want the very best for all students	Serving the students is the highest priority in this school
Students here are caring towards one another	Students here are caring towards one another	The people I work with are willing to help each other even if it means doing something outside their usual activities or job
I am well supported in my learning at school	The school helps me to support my child's learning	Parents' involvement supports learning here
I am able to join in a good range of activities outside the school day	The school offers a good range of opportunities for my child to learn outside the school day	Extra-curricular activity is a valued feature of this school
I have opportunities to learn from people outside school	The involvement of the wider community supports learning here	The involvement of the wider community supports learning here
I feel well prepared for my future	The school makes sure my child is well prepared for their future	I am encouraged to learn and develop myself

(Download combined versions for each stakeholder group from www.flippingschools.net)

3. Where are you trying to get to?

Figure 13 (adapted from Gelsthorpe and West-Burnham 2003) maps a possible spectrum of the elements involved in turning the school inside out against nine dimensions. The spectrum is based on the ideas of bonding (exclusive) culture and bridging (inclusive) culture, which we explored from a more theoretical perspective in chapter 10. It characterises three broad stages of development for each of the nine dimensions, which in total help to turn a school outwards to become more inclusive.

Based on your analysis of where you are now (see pages 180–185), where do you want to be regarding each of these dimensions in one, three or five years' time? What needs to change for that to happen? Which are the dimensions you would choose to start on, and why?

BRIDGING (Inclusive)

Leadership focused on community renewal and social activism.
Families as partners in learning.
Negotiated and relevant curriculum. Focus on cultural capital.
Collaboration with other schools – cooperation not competition.
Fully integrated working with other agencies around community wellbeing.
School as a community resource.
Students widely involved in community activism/leadership.
Teachers and others as social educators.
The school as a centre for social and economic entrepreneurship.

Fully inclusive

Leadership widely distributed and community focused.
Parents as co-educators.
Inclusive curriculum involving 'knowledge-creators'.
Active partnerships with other schools/educational groups.
Positive cooperation with other agencies.
Genuine student leadership developed within the school.
Extended usage of school resources.
Teachers engaged with the community.
The school becoming seen as outward-facing and engaged.

Moving towards inclusion

Leadership focused on school improvement and management.
Parents involved by invitation.
Restricted definition of the curriculum – subject and assessment based.
Limited networking/partnership with other schools.
Functional engagement with other agencies/silos.
Limited student voice.
Restricted access to school resources.
Teachers' roles limited to effective pedagogy.
Minimal entrepreneurial involvement by the school in its communities.

BONDING (Exclusive)

Figure 13: From Bonding to Bridging: A Spectrum of School Engagement and Connectivity

A copy of this can be downloaded from www.flippingschools.net

PART THREE
So What About It?

15. So What Now?

We want an education system based on hope not fear, one that appreciates the humanity of human beings.
(Yong Zhao)

Throughout this book we have been attempting to flesh out a number of key propositions. We have argued that our present model of school accountability is broken. It is no longer fit for purpose because it underestimates the role of genetic, economic, social and family factors on educational outcomes, and overestimates the significance of the school. It is no longer fit for purpose because we have lost sight of the understanding of measurement. We no longer measure what we value but (over-)value what we can measure. It is no longer fit for purpose because it has become over-reliant on top-down compliance and fails to empower leaders, staff, parents or pupils to be their own changemakers.

We believe this analysis is grounded in an established and rapidly expanding base of evidence and research. But we also need to attach a note of caution to that, for the concept of evidence-based (or as we prefer, evidence-informed) practice is in danger of becoming misunderstood and sometimes abused. This is because it is not possible to separate evidence from the exercise of professional judgement and from the values base that underpins that. Gert Biesta (2010) argues that the increasing pursuit of evidence-based practice suffers from three weaknesses or deficits. These are:

- A knowledge deficit: not understanding that relationships between actions and consequences can only ever provide us with possibilities, never with certainties.

- An efficacy deficit: not understanding that in a social domain such as education, interventions do not produce effects in a mechanistic, linear or deterministic way.
- An application deficit: not understanding the work that needs to be done to transform practices in the outside world so that knowledge can begin to work.

He concludes:

> The 'project' of evidence-based practice therefore urgently needs to be rethought in ways that take into consideration the limits of knowledge, the nature of social interaction, the ways in which things can work, the processes of power that are involved in this and, most importantly, the values and normative orientations that constitute social practices such as education. (Biesta 2010, p.501)

Bearing this in mind, we do not claim the evidence we have presented provides proof in any absolute sense. Its meaning rests on values, on relationships and on implementation. The evidence does not in itself tell us what to do, even though it strongly suggests some directions for travel. It is for each school to find the right path for their own context.

Starting on a national journey to address the issues raised in this book does require changes of both mindset and policy at government level. However, much also sits in the hands of school leaders today. Though leaders will need both bravery and canniness to take risks, successful change is entirely possible, even now. It is possible to find a way out of the school improvement cul-de-sac, and we have provided some examples of what this can look like and where it might lead.

The examples we have chosen deliberately do not come from brand new schools, able to create themselves in their own image from the ground up. Our examples are of established and even in some senses 'ordinary' schools, changing even as they continue to function. While one is 'outstanding' in the view of Ofsted, the others have all been classified as 'good' schools. What they share in common is that they have moved beyond purely school-centric thinking towards person-centred and community-centred understandings. As a result, they are in the process of effectively turning themselves inside out through their understanding of the primacy of relationships, the value of each individual, the need to work from shared values and to involve all stakeholders, and their deep recognition of learning beyond the school.

Our argument is that if some schools out there – such as these four schools and their leaders – can make changes in the way they think about accountability, outcomes, purpose and quality and start to do things differently, then there is nothing in principle (except perhaps fear) to stop any other school that wants to do the same. Of course, by 'do the same' we do not mean creating an identical copycat version; we mean that each school should apply the principles and the lessons in their own context following their own professional judgement.

In this final part of this book we will address ourselves primarily to those school leaders who want to take that step, and to those who have begun but want to go further faster. We will try to highlight what we feel are the real priorities for these school leaders in chapter 16. But we will also address ourselves in chapter 17 to the system leaders and education policy-makers who can help or hinder that process.

The essence of the case we have made is that the key to future school improvement and securing the best outcomes for every young person involves a shift of focus towards paying greater attention to the building of social capital. We have suggested that although this has to start within the school, it needs to extend outwards to influence families and communities if the effect is to be long-lasting. The balance between school improvement and community engagement needs to be re-cast to better reflect their respective spheres of influence on educational achievement.

We have used the model of four building blocks to identify what the key elements of this process of change might involve, and we have drawn eight lessons around these building blocks from the practice of four schools in England today. These are all summarised in Table 7.

THE OUTWARD-FACING SCHOOL	LESSONS FROM PRACTICE
A PLACE OF TRUST AND MUTUAL RESPECT	1. Values matter, and in the inside-out school everyone needs to live them. 2. A community does not just happen for an inside-out school. It requires care, commitment, work and planning right from the outset.
A BASE OF VALUE AND VALUES	3. Community, values and curriculum are inextricably intertwined. 4. It is practically possible to make learning both real and personal, even in what might be seen as an orthodox and very large school setting.
AN ENGINE OF ENGAGEMENT AND PARTICIPATION	5. To be willing to engage, people need to feel wanted and that their engagement will be of value in some way, and to see a reason for doing so. 6. Securing effective and reciprocal engagement involves combining structure and organisation with great flexibility, openness and responsiveness.
A HUB OF NETWORKS AND SUPPORT FOR LEARNING	7. Successful leadership in a complex environment, such as a school, involves nurturing an environment for changemakers to emerge. 8. Connected leadership requires perseverance as well as patience, attention to details as well as vision, humility as well as conviction.

Table 7: The Four Building Blocks and Eight Lessons From Practice

None of these lessons from practice offers a series of simple steps to take, and leadership is not in the main like that. The lessons do not amount to a textbook or instruction manual; what they offer is more akin to getting a set of bearings. They can serve as a guide and act as reference points for those seeking to move forwards.

But if we are to take seriously the case for flipping schools inside out, we believe there are important implications for how we go about things, both for school leaders and for those with some responsibility for the wider school system. The next chapters summarise what seem to us to be the priorities.

16. So What Now for School Leadership?

Sometimes you just have to jump off the cliff and learn how to make wings on the way down.

(Ray Bradbury)

The revolution in scientific thinking that introduced the concepts of quantum physics, chaos theory and complexity science provides a powerful model for the paradigm shift in leadership that lies at the heart of our discussion in this book. The quantum paradigm holds that nothing is fixed, events are not predictable, control is an illusion and change is continuous. As such, it lends itself to situations that arise during turbulent times; when there are strong pressures to change, events seem chaotic, objectives have become ambiguous, and order seems to emerge of its own accord and in its own time. This seems to describe today's environment perfectly!

Traditional management theorists see groups as systems through which goals are accomplished and, as such, they tend towards hierarchy. Causality is linear. An organisation's internal dynamic affects members, but only leaders are seen as affecting the internal dynamic. Most traditional leadership paradigms, including traditional school-improvement thinking, fit that mould.

The quantum perspective, on the other hand, emphasises free-flowing interaction, co-acting with moral purpose to make a positive difference in people's lives. From this perspective an organisation and its members are viewed as interconnected, energetic beings, enhanced by collaboration and interaction, where the connections are non-linear and non-hierarchical. In other words, it is less of an organisation and more of a community.

What does it mean to be a leader in such an environment, while at the same time being responsible for a school which has very clear and fixed responsibilities as an organisation? Here are seven possible starting points for school leaders looking to turn their schools and communities inside out.

Get the central focus right

The first implication of our message for school leadership lies in the need to re-frame its central focus. This is the transforming step Sir John Timpson took in his own business all those years ago (see chapter 3). It means putting people and the quality of relationships first and centre; not in some soft, cosy, cuddly way, but in terms of trust and respect combined with clear intent. For Timpson, that meant removing layers of supervision to ensure each member of staff is empowered to give great service to each customer every time, whatever it takes. The role of leadership is to enable that to happen, securing it with the right people, the right training and the right culture.

For leaders of schools, this means removing barriers to learning by ensuring each member of staff can do the right thing for this child at this moment, whatever it takes.

Work with stakeholders to develop shared values

The 'right' thing is of course a value judgement. That is why a shared base of core values is such a crucial element. The nature of those values means they apply to everyone across the organisation. In the case of schools, that means all leaders, all staff and all pupils, but the values should also aim to reach beyond the school to become shared with families and communities.

The reason for this was put well to us by Nick Lewis, head at Fairfield High School. He described how the school had succeeded in establishing a culture and climate which gave each pupil the space to be themselves and to thrive. He spoke about how difficult one autistic boy found life when he moved on to post-16 education in another school. The boy had said afterwards: 'It was a really difficult transition. I thought the world would be like Fairfield, but it isn't.' This presented Nick with a challenge:

> The more you create something that's special, the more you have to up the energy into promoting that, or trying to replicate that into the world beyond, as well as giving those students themselves an onward moral purpose, to be agents of change beyond Fairfield.

There is little point in enabling students to advance in the world through education and move away from their community if one effect is to completely denude those communities of their capacity for future growth. Nor would it make sense to support such students to remain in their communities if the effect of schooling is to turn them in a real sense into 'outsiders' because of their changed outlook and experience.

This is in part the tension provocatively examined by David Goodhart (2017) in his book *The Road to Somewhere*. He sees the British in particular (though his analysis perhaps has wider significance) as belonging to a nation to a large degree split into two tribes, which he terms 'Somewheres' and 'Anywheres'. The Anywheres dominate our culture and represent a worldview for (in the main) successful individuals who care about society. This worldview places a high value on autonomy, mobility and novelty, along with much less value on group identity, tradition and such nationalistic emblems as faith, flag and family. The Somewheres, in contrast, are more socially conservative and communitarian by instinct. They are moderately nationalistic and feel uncomfortable about many aspects of cultural and economic change, such as mass immigration, an achievement society in which they struggle to achieve, the reduced status of non-graduate employment, and more fluid gender roles. The Anywheres have been the dominant cultural force, though not necessarily in a majority by number.

The overlooking and neglect of the Somewheres by the Anywheres over a long period of time was, Goodhart argues, one significant contributory factor in the Brexit vote. But, more importantly for this discussion, the role of education – including the pressure on the expansion of higher education – has had the unintended effect of hollowing out established communities and taking young people with ability away from them, by encouraging a perception that moving away from your roots to go to university is *the* measure of success.

It feels to us as if he makes an important point. This is in no way an argument against ensuring all young people get the best life chances possible (as they determine them to be). It is to say that the understanding of shared values between families, communities and school needs far more attention than it has been given in the past.

Maintain an ongoing dialogue

Arriving at such shared values is not a one-off job to be ticked off a list. To be alive, values have to be continually re-visited, understood and interpreted. They have to form the subject of ongoing dialogue and reflection across the school and its communities, allowing everyone to understand and interpret their meaning in the context of the moment. This involves extended conversations with each other about the world students will enter, about what students will need to be successful in the twenty-first century, and then how that might impact on what they do in school. This is, incidentally, a vital (though often under-emphasised) form of professional development for staff and curriculum development for students.

There is an important sense in which this does not make for consistency (that feature beloved of those involved with quality assurance), for the resulting judgements will be often be context-specific and individual. But leaders like Nick Lewis are clear:

> I'm not sure I want [consistency]. I want people to have the ability to be inconsistent, and through that to discover new and novel things, to help move things forward.

Maintaining an ongoing dialogue means leaders need to be skilled at managing disagreement (and indeed mistrust), as well being able to handle conflict creatively. If successful, however, it will allow you to tell the story of what happens in your school; how that reflects the way you all see the fundamental purpose of education; and how that will prepare students to understand and shape their futures in modern Britain and in a global society.

Build a shared framework of accountability

Shared values are not enough if they just remain warm words. Are they being realised in practice? This, in turn, means having a shared understanding of accountability and a framework by which to gauge success. In addition to the government's accountability measures, which cannot be ignored even if they should not dominate your thinking, define performance measures with your stakeholders that demonstrate whether the school is achieving its *own* vision and aims. Start to build everyone's capacity to contribute to, use and interrogate data to create a rich picture.

The key features of such an approach are that it:

- is an on-going process and commitment, not a one-off or relatively rare special event
- puts learning at the centre of its interest
- meshes both qualitative and quantitative information to arrive at judgements and enable the asking of powerful questions
- is rooted in the effective partnership and understanding of all key stakeholders
- uses processes that are clear and open to all concerned
- is planned in advance and its results are integral to future development planning
- provides some knowledge at any one time about the general state of the school, with more detailed information being available on agreed specific aspects
- makes realistic and manageable demands on time for all involved.

Get the curriculum right

When human values lie at the heart of the school, they must also drive the curriculum.

That means moving assessment out of the driving seat and restoring it to its rightful place as a servant – not a master – for both learners and teachers. School leaders already have the power to do that for their staff, their students and their communities. But they need to exercise that power (having secured the support of their stakeholders), and the more that is not an isolated or individual act by just one school leader, the more powerful if becomes.

Of course, school leaders cannot ignore government requirements and inspection frameworks. Rather they have to become what Rae Snape calls 'pragmaticians', that is educators who 'train for the test but teach for life'. They are those who, at the end of the day, 'want our children to be happy today, fulfilled in the future, and able to make their world an even better place'. They have the confidence to take account of (but not be driven by) those external demands, because they follow a higher purpose.

The notion of 'teaching for life' means having a clear rationale for the curriculum that amounts to much more than just subscribing to a set of subject disciplines or the transmission of a body of subject knowledge, as is clearly evident in the Spinney case study (see pages 113–117).

There is much to be learnt from early-years practice, which is applicable to the learning of children and young people whatever their age. The four over-arching principles set out in the statutory framework for the early years foundation stage (DfE 2017), have equal relevance for all stages of schooling:

- Every child is a unique child, who is constantly learning and can be resilient, capable, confident and self-assured.
- Children learn to be strong and independent through positive relationships.
- Children learn and develop well in enabling environments, in which their experiences respond to their individual needs and there is a strong partnership between practitioners and parents and/or carers.
- Children develop and learn in different ways.

From those principles flow a number of important messages with which leaders across all phases of schooling need to grapple:

- Treating each learner as an individual.
- Making careful use of structured observation and assessment by teachers.
- Creating carefully planned environments which support and challenge independent learners.

It is sometimes claimed that while this is all very well for children in the early-years stage, when they 'only really play', it is not possible or appropriate once the child reaches 'proper' school, when there is 'work' that needs to be done and tests that need to be passed. In our view, nothing could be further from the truth and this misassumption is one of the major errors of a school-centric approach.

Equally, there is thinking grounded in the secondary curriculum that has a wider application for all ages. The Edge Foundation, drawing on a wide range of evidence from international research, identifies three principles for deeper learning to address what they believe are current systemic weaknesses in English education:

- **Making learning relevant to real life:** this involves breaking down subject boundaries and teaching through a real-world lens.
- **Developing transferable skills:** this means equipping young people with the skills they need for further study, work and life.
- **Involving employers and the community:** this includes involving local employers and the community in developing the future plan for the school and its curriculum delivery.

Although the approach taken will vary according to the age and stage of each child, the goal at every stage is 'a knowledge-engaged curriculum that matches and synchronises knowledge and skills development' (The Edge Foundation 2019, p.18).

Such a curriculum is not a pragmatic or instrumentalist response to national accountability measures. It has a bold vision that is rooted in person-centred values and also reflects the communities which the school serves. It is a curriculum that builds character and resilience, and inspires and enables young people to achieve as well as to be successful, rounded people. It challenges perceptions of innate ability and low expectation. And it has involved the whole school community in its ongoing design and development.

Engage with all families as equal partners

Although we have argued throughout this book for the need to engage with all stakeholders, there is a particular need to address the engagement of families because of their role and influence in educating their children. This goes well beyond the simplistic notions of parental choice that have governed national policy for several decades, which revolve around 'choosing' which school your children attend.

Instead, we think engaging with families means:

- Developing systematic and continuous engagement right from the very beginning.
- Looking to include all families, not just the advantaged.
- Recognising that children's learning extends beyond the school.
- Shifting our mindset from doing for and to, towards actively co-creating opportunities to engage with parents.

None of this is easy. Parents are also affected (or indeed bombarded) by the deficit model of education and schools promoted by some policy-makers and the media. Many carry with them their own negative associations of school and of 'authority' more generally. But by building supportive and sympathetic relationships very carefully from the earliest moment of contact – relationships which are based on mutual trust and respect; a clear, shared focus on supporting children's learning; recognising each other's contributions; and by making changes in day-to-day practice to match – the four schools we studied (and they are not alone) have shown that a new partnership can be built.

However, for that to happen, schools will also need to make space within their professional development strategy for all staff to work on this in order to support the shifts in mindset and skills that are needed.

Weave plenty of webs

Both Robert Putnam and Thomas Maak have chosen the image of web-weavers to describe the leadership now needed if we are to do things differently. In Putnam's view:

> Reweaving social webs will depend in part on the efforts of dedicated local leaders who choose to pursue their goals ... through the sometimes slow, frequently fractious, and profoundly transformative route of social capital building. (Putnam and Feldstein 2003, p.294)

The idea of 'reweaving social webs' is a very powerful image. Picture a social loom with the geographical, social and economic components of the warp being changed by the values and relationships of the weft. Change either and the cloth is very different, and the permutations are almost endless.

If the building of social capital holds the key to long-term future school improvement, then it falls to the school leaders of today to start to make the change through their focus on values and relationships. Such leaders see the school and its communities as mutual resources. They actively look for opportunities to draw on these to support the learning and wellbeing of children, young people and their families. As community leaders, they take responsibility beyond the statutory boundaries. They encourage, motivate and create networks, enabling people to work together on a shared vision which makes a positive difference to the lives of children and young people.

In taking up that challenge, remember that no school or community is the same as another. So start from where you are at and remember that no-one else has your answers.

17. So What Now for System Leadership?

Turning schools inside out involves leadership that works beyond the historical confines and boundaries of the individual school. One of the great challenges for school leaders still having to operate within the demands of GERM (see page 14) is to change their personal mindscape, or mental map, to accommodate assumptions, strategies and behaviours that are based on collaboration and cooperation, and which involve working and thinking interdependently.

The basis for any model of system leadership is the integration of the component parts of the system both vertically and laterally, so that all elements are able to engage interdependently on equal terms. This implies, of course, a focus on values, norms and shared purpose. However, to enable schools to radically rethink their relationships requires a focus on the how as well as the what and why. This means developing systems and structures that are replicable at micro, mezzo and macro levels, and across geographical and social boundaries.

We need to remember that working across the system is very different to working across a school. Indeed, one of the major factors that leads to the failure of systems-based approaches is the failure to think beyond parochial interests. This applies as much to a few schools exploring working together in an academy trust as it does to government negotiations at an international level. History is littered with examples of self-interest leading to a breakdown in relationships because of a lack of empathy, the inability to collaborate, or a closed mindset.

There is, as we have seen, much that school leaders can do within their own individual situations by flipping their schools inside out, and this can be magnified through collaborative sharing with other leaders engaged in similar work. This progress made by individual leaders is important, and helps to show other schools what can be possible. But the weaknesses of school-centric thinking and misjudged accountability that we have described and evidenced run too deep to rely solely on individual change. Systemic change is needed as well as school change; indeed, the two are mutually reinforcing. Therefore, common systems and structures are needed to facilitate effective interaction to lead to significant and sustainable change.

Blood transfusions only work if donor and recipient have the same blood group. Incompatible blood groups are literally poisonous, and the body can reject non-matching transplants. System leadership can be similarly compromised by incompatible approaches. The interaction between schools is often compromised by low skill levels in terms of communication, a belief in the importance of autonomy, and the potentially inhibiting focus on competition and transactional relationships (for instance, selling rather than sharing resources). What is lacking at the moment is any real consensus as to the nature of systemic thinking beyond the individual school or trust.

So what is it that system leaders can do, and what sort of policy development could contribute to an environment in which change can be accelerated across the board?

From organisation to community to 'village'

One of our most significant social archetypes is the village; or rather, the idealised image that dominates how village life is perceived from literature and drama to the hyperbole of estate agents. Memoirs such as *Lark Rise to Candleford* and *Cider with Rosie*, as well as novels such as *The Darling Buds of May*, present a similarly bucolic and utopian view of village life. In spite of a murder rate to compare with any urban ghetto, the village of Midsomer in the television series *Midsomer Murders* has all of the stereotypes of modern middle-class village life: fetes, drama productions, and the pivotal role of the key events in the church's year. This is the England of Vaughn Williams and John Constable, in dramatic antithesis to life in modern urban environments. This idealistic view is often advanced by people who have no experience of the wage slavery of agricultural workers, or the limited access to healthcare, social services and public transport (along with the quasi-feudal social relationships) that were also common-place features of life in rural England before the industrial revolution.

Pinker (2014) argues that to build the village effect you need a 'community of real friends that you see in the real world'. She goes on to suggest:

> ... the evidence is clear. From the Chicago heat wave to hurricanes Sandy and Katrina and the earthquakes in Japan and India, those most likely to make it had people in their circle who cared enough to check up on them and lend a hand. Those who were isolated – during or after the crisis – were more likely to die. (Pinker 2014, p.290)

In her conclusion to *The Village Effect*, she reinforces the centrality of social contact and stresses the importance of access to authentic social relationships that, for her, are enabled and enhanced by living in an authentic community:

> We – both men and women – are happier, healthier and more resistant to disease and despair if we satisfy the need for meaningful human contact. Our loads seem lighter, the hills literally less steep. Genuine social interaction is a force of nature. (Pinker 2014, p.309)

From the compiling of the Domesday Book in 1086 to the enclosing of common land in the eighteenth century, the average number of people living in an English village was about 150, according to Dunbar (2010). He goes on to cite numerous examples of what has become known as 'Dunbar's number': the persistence of 150 as the optimum size for any human enterprise. For example, the Hutterites and Amish communities have average community sizes of 110. They split their communities once they reach 150 because at that point it becomes difficult to manage the behaviour of the community by peer pressure alone.

> What keeps the community together is a sense of mutual obligation and reciprocity ... Since their whole ethos is against having hierarchies and police forces, they prefer to split their communities before they get to that point. (Dunbar 2010, p.27)

It seems reasonable to draw a tentative conclusion that there might be a high correlation between the size of a community and the behaviour of its members. So, group size becomes a significant variable in building engagement and securing commitment. Perhaps – to paraphrase one of the most potent clichés in this context – it takes an extended family, a village community, and multiple interactive networks to help raise a child.

Re-imagine each school as if it was a village

We would therefore argue that the starting point for systemic change lies in seeing the school as more akin to a village. Most villages are a microcosm of society as a whole, in particular in terms of the ratio of ages from the very young to the very old. In his discussion of childhood in traditional societies, Diamond describes how children of all ages play together:

> The young children gain from being socialised not only by adults but also by older children, while the older children acquire experience in caring for younger children ... Western teenagers are sub optimal parents because of inexperience. (Diamond 2012, p.201)

Diamond goes on to identify a range of outcomes characteristic of growing up in traditional societies:

- The emotional security, self-confidence, curiosity and autonomy of members of small-scale societies, not only as adults but already as children.
- People spend more time talking to each other.
- No time is spent on passive entertainment, such as television and video games.
- The precocious development of social skills.
- The proximity of caretakers.

He concludes that Western society discourages the development of these characteristics 'by ranking and grading our children, and constantly telling them what to do' (Diamond 2012, p.208).

It would be naïve in the extreme to argue that Western childhoods should be more similar to those experienced by children in traditional societies in New Guinea, but there might be alternative principles to consider and models to explore and adapt. The characteristics listed above are surely desirable in any context, and would seem both appropriate and relevant to the growth of cultural and social capital. However, not all schools function in such a way as to enhance personal and social effectiveness. In fact, the culture in some schools might well be seen as hostile to the principles outlined above.

A more village-like approach can bring a number of advantages:

- An enhanced sense of belonging, a feeling of security, and being known, respected and valued as an individual.
- The development of a shared language and common vocabulary to enhance meaningful dialogue.
- The potential for older members of families and the village to act as mentors to support learning (particularly in regard to literacy and interventions to support meta-cognition).
- Developing a culture of student leadership, with responsibilities across families, villages and the wider community.
- Securing consensus about social norms, behaviours and relationships.

There are some primary and secondary schools that have been designed to facilitate social interaction and successful learning. All too often, however, schools are essentially a series of corridors with rooms off them designed to accommodate 30 young people and one adult. With the addition, in many secondary schools, of tables set out in rows, it becomes clear that this is the architecture of teaching rather than of learning. It is equally clear that the organisational structure is essentially linear and hierarchical based on age, perpetuating the myth that learning takes place in homogeneous cohorts. (For obvious reasons, special schools do seem to be more effective in the appropriate use of space and the focus on relationships.)

Many secondary schools are structured with parallel systems of academic departments and the classic year-based pastoral system. Quite apart from the obvious potential tensions between academic and pastoral systems, the use of age-related cohorts appears to go against every principle that has been explored in this discussion.

If the concept of the Dunbar number is accepted as an indicator of potential community effectiveness and the 'village effect', then the size of a school might be a significant factor. The School Census for 2018 shows that the average size of an English secondary school is 948 students, while primary schools average 281 pupils and special schools 114 pupils (Department for Education 2018). While many children thrive in the prevailing model of schools as organisations, for a significant number of children school is an alien way of life. Many of the issues with mental health, engagement and wellbeing might be related to the poor emotional engagement with school for some children. If form does follow function, then it might be that the current form of many schools is not wholly fit for purpose.

Hypothetically, achieving a better structure might draw on the following principles, using the broad numerical groupings in the Dunbar number model:

- Students are allocated to a family (or team) of between five and eight students (bearing in mind the Ringelmann effect),[30] drawn from all year groups, with senior students as leaders.
- Three to four families make up a clan, with one or two adults as mentors.
- Four to five clans make up a 'learning village'.
- Six learning villages make up a learning community/school.

30. The Ringelmann effect is the tendency for individual members of a group to become increasingly less productive as the size of their group increases (Ringelmann 1913).

The key functions of the family and the clan can be best summed up as building social capital and ensuring the integrity of the social and learning experiences of every student.

A significant positive outcome for the approach outlined above is that it makes it possible to embed some of the best strategies to support effective learning into all aspects of the school's structures and processes. For example, the Education Endowment Foundation Toolkit supports collaborative learning, which would fit naturally with the notion of a family- based model – form follows function in order to embed learning relationships:

> The impact of collaborative approaches on learning is consistently positive. However, the size of impact varies, so it is important to get the detail right. (Education Endowment Foundation, no date)

The Toolkit also endorses the potential of peer tutoring:

> Overall, the introduction of peer tutoring approaches appears to have a positive impact on learning, with an average positive effect equivalent to approximately five additional months' progress. Studies have identified benefits for both tutors and tutees, and for a wide range of age groups.

Seeing the school more in terms of a village also implies that it is an inclusive community. It is open and welcoming; works to create a sense of willingness to engage with social and cultural change; and accepts those from different cultures and systems as they are. Key characteristics of an inclusive community have to be kindness, care and respect for difference. While there are dysfunctional villages that are hostile to newcomers, there are more that actively seek engagement and opportunities for renewal based on shared wellbeing and collective will.

Strengthen lateral connections

Schools are not the only agencies concerned with families, children and young people. One of the potentially negative effects of the reforms of the public sector and the erosion (if not actual loss) of the Beveridge principles of a welfare state, has been the loss of an overarching set of coherent principles to inform the wellbeing of society as a whole.

Instead, we have a fragmented and highly diversified quasi-partnership of a wide range of providers, with an uneasy relationship between maintained and privatised services. Responses to the challenges this poses in terms of securing equity, social mobility, cultural and social capital and wellbeing now have to be focused on:

- Moving from autonomous professional silos to client-focused services.
- Developing services that work on an integrated basis.
- Supporting professionals working interdependently with parity of esteem.

It might seem completely non-contentious to argue for integrated and holistic services for children. However, a series of tragedies involving the death of children through neglect or violence points to the inadequacy of current arrangements. The abuse and neglect of children remains one of the most grievous aspects of life in modern Britain.

One of the answers has to lie in far greater coordination of children's services, with education playing a central role. Schools are at the heart of their communities, with virtually every child being known by a school. This points to a pivotal role for the education system in securing wellbeing for every child and young person.

The aspiration to such integrated thinking across a community faces a number of significant barriers:

- **Limited as opposed to extended professionalism.** Essentially this is the narrow focus found in all professions as a manifestation of a closed definition of their role as a professional. It finds expression in such statements as 'my job is to teach history – not to be a social worker'.
- **The development of a specialist language that limits the understanding of the client.** Professionals develop arcane and esoteric language in order to secure control of their work and create dependency. Medicine can be an example of this.

- **Professions becoming self-referential.** They develop and control bureaucratic systems that validate and justify prevailing practice, irrespective of the needs of clients.
- **Competition between and within professions.** Understandably, when resources are scarce, competition for status and resources can dominate relationships, and interactions are compromised in the struggle to secure resources.
- **Perceived hierarchy and power.** Professionals are often working in silos with parallel accountability and competing professional identities, with hierarchical status and the pursuit or maintenance of power determining working relationships.
- **The territorial imperative.** This is one of the most common manifestations of the identity of a flock, a herd, a pack, or a human group with a shared interest. Teachers often make their classrooms an expression of their ownership of their patch of territory.

The British mentality is very prone to some (perhaps even most) of these characteristics, from the drive to create an empire to pride in one's garden. A sense of place is an important component of social capital, but there is a large gap between belonging and owning. Equally, the ambition and pride associated with becoming a professional are vitally important to securing commitment and engagement, but that must be to the system not the personal fiefdom.

Lucy Crehan provides us with an example of collaboration and cooperation at work from another country:

> Finnish schools do much more than teaching children ... I was privileged to meet the school psychologist, the school social worker and the study counsellor ... but, unfortunately, didn't have time to meet the school dentist, school nurse, speech therapist or family counsellor. (Crehan 2016, p.28)

Crehan goes on to describe the working of the multidisciplinary group known as the child welfare team. The team, which is a legal requirement for every school in the Finland, reviews the progress of every child on an annual cycle. What is important here is not the issue of being under-resourced, although that is obviously significant, but rather the values and mindset that are required to work in an interdisciplinary culture. Another crucial difference about this team is that it is concerned with the wellbeing of the child holistically, engaging with all of the variables that influence happiness and success.

Both our schools and the system within which they operate now need to strengthen the lateral connections that would make such teamwork easier. It begins with a mindset that is open to the reallocation of resources and responsibilities.

Re-model our approach to leadership development for all

The training and development of teachers and leaders in schools has for many years been school-centred. But if community-focused education is to work, then a new repertoire of qualities, behaviours and knowledge will be required for all staff. The principles and lessons that we have explored, especially in Part Three, require a fundamental reorientation of long-accepted beliefs and practices, as well as the development of a new mindset, underpinned by an alternative set of components necessary to succeed when working in the system and when building community.

Of course, there will still be a need for teachers with deep subject knowledge and a portfolio of pedagogic strategies committed to pupil learning and achievement. Equally, we now need leaders who are confident in their professional values, with a clear sense of strategic priorities and high-quality social relationships. Success in turning schools inside out depends on a great deal of rethinking of roles, values and relationships. Thus, leading a community is very much about leading change, and in particular helping people to adjust their personal mindsets.

Imagine a situation where an elderly lady, in good health and still socially active but increasingly frail, is no longer able to manage her home where she has lived since her husband died several years before. She resists every invitation and blandishment to move to residential care, arguing that she does not want to leave her home. Linsky and Lawrence (2011) refer to this as the tension between technical problems and adaptive challenges. Technical problems are generally non-contentious; adaptive challenges have personal and emotional significance – they are matters of value, not fact. Working at the system level involves, for some, a radical reorientation of many assumptions and checking of values.

Gilchrist argues that networking in itself is neutral:

> [Networking is] the creation, maintenance and use of links and relationships between individuals and/or organisations. Networking itself is a neutral tool – it can be used for a variety of purposes, selfish, altruistic, or simply to get things done. (Gilchrist 2005, p.55)

Gilchrist then goes on to argue that networking across the community involves certain key values including 'equity, empowerment and participation'. It therefore becomes necessary to identify a range of leadership characteristics suited to responding to adaptive challenges and networking at system level.

Most of the components in Table 8 are equally appropriate to working and leading in a single institution. However, some become more widely significant according to context and the extent to which a particular project or strategy is contentious.

Of course, it is unrealistic and a counsel of perfection to expect that one person will display all of the characteristics outlined in Table 8. It is equally inappropriate to have a hierarchy of capability where some characteristics are reserved for senior staff. System and community leadership requires shared or total leadership, and leadership in depth. Age and status are no guarantee of empathy or sensitivity.

Qualities	Behaviours	Knowledge
Moral confidence/ inclusivity/equity Trust/integrity/ consistency Courage Entrepreneurship Imagination/creativity Challenge Empathy/emotional literacy Diplomacy/sensitivity Optimism/resilience Humility	Consensus building Networking Team development Building coalitions Conflict management Risk taking Analytical thinking Problem solving Effective communication Negotiation/listening	School-improvement strategies Closing the gap Systems thinking Sensitivity to context Political insights Policy initiatives Leading change Consultancy skills HR strategies Project management

Table 8: The Components of Collaborative and Systems Leadership

What is needed now is a model of professional development that is focused on people being able to internalise new models and approaches, which helps them to change their mindset and, through that, their behaviour. This involves much more than a new suite of skills and strategies that can be presented in a set of PowerPoint slides or wrapped up in a training manual. But it may work if approaches to learning are employed that facilitate understanding and enable application.

> An individual understands a concept, skill, theory, or domain of knowledge to the extent that he or she can apply it. This formulation entails an acid test for understanding: posing to students a topic or theme or demonstration that they have never before encountered, and determining what sense they can make of those phenomena. An individual who possesses relevant understanding will be able to draw on appropriate concepts. (Gardner 1999, p.119)

There are two models of learning for understanding that are particularly relevant to this context: firstly, action learning approaches, and secondly, mentoring and coaching. These approaches share a number of characteristics that make them most appropriate for engaging across the community and at system level:

- The process is owned and driven by the learner.
- The focus is on learning through social interaction.
- The key agent is dialogue.
- The emphasis is on integrating theory and practice.

Action learning is a practice-orientated, problem-solving model that works through collaborative approaches. It is based on the principle of 'learning by doing'. It combines a focus on shared problem solving, and personal and group learning. It is a powerful vehicle for improving performance, developing practice and supporting innovation. Because it works through genuine issues, it is perceived to be both relevant and developmental. It requires a systematic and disciplined approach and, most distinctively, the active intervention of a coach or adviser to provide support and ensure the integrity of the learning process.

Rather than talking about INSET or CPD, David Hargreaves argues for 'joint practice development' as the answer to the problem of getting professional development to actually make a difference (Hargreaves 2012, p.8). The power of Hargreaves' model is that it builds collaboration right into teaching and learning, as well as into leadership of the improvement process. Effective and high-impact professional learning is rooted in a model of collaboration. This strengthens the case for collaboration in that it is not just structural but it is also embedded in learning and professional relationships.

Joint practice development is:

- a **joint** activity, in which two or more people interact with and influence one another (in contrast to the non-interactive, unilateral character of much conventional 'sharing of good practice')
- an activity that focuses on professional **practice**, i.e. what people do, not merely what they know

- a **development** of the practice, not simply a transfer of it from one person or place to another (thus it is a form of school or community improvement).

Successful action learning is driven by practitioners with the support of an adviser or coach in order to maximise the effectiveness of the process. Most of us develop language as young children through an intensive one-to-one relationship; we learn to drive on the same basis. The greatest artists and musicians have usually had their innate ability developed in the same way. The concept of apprenticeship was central to most trades for centuries, and reflects the balance of mentoring and coaching in effective learning and development.

The transition from apprentice to master craftsperson reflects the movement from coaching to mentoring. The boundaries between coaching and mentoring are the subject of significant partisan debate. In reality of course they are at different positions on the continuum of helping relationships, with a spectrum from prescription to non-directive counselling. The relationship between coaching and mentoring is summarised in Table 9.

Coaching	Mentoring
A focused intervention or series of interventions to provide explicit support in developing specific skills, techniques and strategies.	A sustained, one-to-one relationship based on trust, in which the mentor actively supports the learner to build capacity to enhance personal effectiveness.

Table 9: Coaching and Mentoring

The components of effective coaching can then be seen as reviewing and considering the following:

- The clarification of the learner's working situation and developmental priorities.
- Personal wellbeing; physical and mental health.
- Securing supporting evidence; reflection and review.

- Feedback on actual performance based on observations, analysis and reflection.
- The implementation of strategies to support problem solving or to enhance performance, such as skill building, setting challenges, providing advice, demonstrating techniques or removing barriers.
- Feedback on progress, recognition and reinforcement of success, and the introduction of alternative strategies if necessary.
- Consolidation and challenge.
- Encouraging reflexivity.

The combination of joint practice development and coaching has the potential to create a culture of learning that applies to all members of the community. Equally, it offers the possibility of creating a common experience of learning that is available to all, thus promoting and sustaining one dimension of the principles and practice of securing equity. Coaching, in particular, has significant potential in supporting the development of cultural capital and empowering the most vulnerable and disadvantaged.

Developing system leadership is about growing to scale – building the community in a proportionate and appropriate way, notably by growing capacity relative to resources. As the system becomes more complex, so the need for leadership becomes more vital as collective capacity increases.

The integrity of the process of turning the school inside out is contingent on rethinking historical patterns of working and their associated attitudes, norms and expectations. Such rethinking has to include the interaction of the micro, the mezzo and the macro – the school as well as the wider system – in such a way that change is reciprocal and mutual.

Re-think our approach to accountability and measurement, and seek public acceptance and understanding for this

Community action has to be based on a model of accountability that is primarily focused on two parallel and interdependent factors. Firstly, the extent to which the action actually works (measured by the impact made in terms of desired outcomes); and secondly, the extent to which the project reinforces and embeds community values and relationships in such a way that task and process are enhanced.

Accountability thus has to combine efficiency (value for money) with effectiveness (achievement of desired outcomes), with both of these aspects understood to function within an agreed moral framework. True accountability is as concerned with values and relationships as with financial probity.

Accountability will only make a difference if it is based on a number of key assumptions:

- It is part of a school-improvement strategy that reflects collaborative partnerships and community engagement.
- It is based on valid and reliable evidence that combines qualitative and quantitative data, and which identifies significant variables and respective levels of responsibility.
- Stakeholders have a voice in both the design and implementation of the evaluation process.
- There are explicit strategies to implement the findings of the accountability process.
- Possible rewards or sanctions do not compromise the integrity of the process. In other words, there is a presumption of integrity and trust.

There are two specific aspects of accountability that are particularly pertinent to community leadership and relationships across the system. Firstly, accountability has to be seen as part of a learning process. Secondly, it must focus on prevention rather than cure. In other words, it is about stopping things going wrong rather than putting them right after they have gone wrong.

Effective, high-performing communities base their improvement on open and shared opportunities for learning in what Etienne Wenger (1998) calls a 'community of practice'. These are the multiple sets of relationships and social interactions that constitute the basis on which we work, engage with our families, and interact with other communities. It is helpful to think of any collaborative enterprise as a constellation of communities. To make a difference, accountability has to recognise and respect the various alternative perspectives at work.

The micro (the school or village) has to be reflected in the macro (the multi-academy trust or district) and vice versa. Accountability must exemplify the principle of form following function. For the purposes of this discussion, the function is securing equity through person- and community-centred learning.

Such accountability has to serve as the basis for development and improvement, not as a bureaucratic chore. One of the foundation principles of any true community is that it works to prevent failure. It involves moving the culture of a team or department from reaction to anticipation and intervention. There are numerous examples of this approach in everyday life. The best way to avoid a heart attack is to stop smoking, not to invest in more cardiac surgeons.

Likewise, the best way to close the education achievement gap and so move towards equity is to prevent children from failing. That means actively challenging poor and inappropriate performance, which in turn means identifying, defining and embedding appropriate performance. While there are a range of strategies and techniques that can help to manage the problem of variation, what matters is that such interventions are reinforced and corroborated by a culture of prevention. In other words, it is not just what we do, it is the way that things are done.

A simple but highly significant example of prevention is vaccination in childhood. The falling numbers of parents who are agreeing to have their children vaccinated points to a very real danger of diseases such as mumps, measles and rubella becoming common again. Vaccination against smallpox has virtually eradicated the disease. We need to 'vaccinate' children against academic failure. Growing up in a caring and literate family in a 'village' of high social capital takes us a long way towards moving from find-and-fix towards predict-and-prevent. In understanding that lies the real future for systemic improvement.

18. A Final Word

School improvement that is not also matched by a strategy for community engagement is no longer fit for purpose. School improvement that bases itself purely on flawed numerical measures and does not take proper account of broader outcomes, such as personal and social development and wellbeing, has now become dangerous and damaging. School improvement that fails to understand the difference between organisation and community cannot now take us to the levels of excellence and equity we need.

We hope you are convinced of this. The children and young people we are educating today face, as a generation, a time of greater challenge – personal, societal and global – than any of us (certainly in developed countries) have experienced. It may well be unprecedented in scale in recorded history. The combination of environmental, societal and technological change have the capacity to destroy both the species and the planet.

This is not inevitable, but it is certainly the case that we are currently losing the race very badly, and much we have taken for granted needs to change fast if we are to turn that around. In a pair of blogs, Michael Fullan (2019a,b) draws on the work of evolutionary biologist David Sloan Wilson to argue it is we, as educators and school leaders, who hold the key to success.

According to Sloan Wilson:

> most evolutionary theory tells us that goodness can evolve, but only when special conditions are met. That's why we must become wise managers of evolutionary processes. Otherwise evolution takes us where we don't want to go. (Wilson 2019, pp.13–14)

Wilson argues that evolution occurs both within a population of individuals but also within a population of groups. Within both of these populations, there is a variation in their propensity for good or evil. Neither is intrinsically good. Moreover, tribalism, where the needs of leaders drive choices, makes people do bad things, or at least not commit to good things for humanity as a whole. For good to flourish, the special conditions which can allow that to happen are crucial.

His solution is to find ways to combine the strengths of a small group with the necessity to connect more widely:

> If you're not surrounded by nurturing others, who know you by your actions, then it will not be possible to thrive as an individual. We must consciously seek to create small groups that benefit individuals as well as society as a whole.

This is strongly resonant of the thoughts of Derek Morrell about the importance of inculcating both individuality and interdependence, cited at the start of chapter 11. It also links to John Macmurray's view of personhood and Michael Fielding's view of the school as a person-centred learning community, also explored in chapter 11. It is in essence what we have called a village-like approach to school and system leadership.

In his two blogs, Fullan argues that it is only educators who are well positioned (though not yet employed) to bring about the change that is now needed. That is not to minimise the need for political action on climate change, or on the many other issues that we face. But education is the only way to learn about the world, as we – through and with our students – change it for the better.

We agree with Fullan's viewpoint. It may be no exaggeration to say that schools and the people who work in them may hold the future of the species in their hands. At one level, though, we do not have to wait to be 'employed' to get on with this. Even if the critical nature of the situation does require a systemic response as well, we can each still make a start.

For this to happen, we do need to shift from seeing the school primarily as an organisation to seeing it primarily as a community. We have to move away from school-centric thinking towards a community-centred, learner-focused mindset. And that means we also need to focus more on collaboration than competition, more on building trust than having control, and, above all, more on learning than teaching.

We do not underestimate the task. But this is why flipping schools – in the sort of ways that we hope you have clearly seen throughout this book are strongly research- and evidence-informed, clearly rooted in human values, and eminently possible in practice – is now such a flipping urgent and vital need.

Acknowledgements

This book began life with a challenge, and there have indeed been moments in its journey to the printed page when it felt as if it might be a challenge too far to find the right words, and the right mix of theory, evidence and practice to give it shape. But as it started to evolve, the challenge turned to excitement. Gradually the pieces started to fit together. At the same time, the need and urgency for what we wanted to say became ever clearer to us. We sincerely hope we have been able to communicate all that to you.

Whether we have succeeded or not, nothing would have been possible without the leaders of schools and businesses who responded to our enquiries, and gave so generously of their time to open up their organisations and to share their thinking and practice, their failures and their successes. To Farina Ackerman, Rachel Clay, Edel Cronin, Kate Farrell, Sally Lees, Nick Lewis, Rae Snape, Caroline Skingsley, Sir John Timpson and Michaela Viola, we are hugely indebted.

Our thanks go too to Charles Fadel for giving us the nudge, through his insightful probing and with that initial challenge, to get on and write the book. And we have received huge encouragement along the way, particularly from Clive Corbett, Ingrid Cox, Brian Lightman and Olly Newton, all of whom have taken time to look at early drafts and to share suggestions and ideas for improvement. Our deep thanks to each, and to our editor Harriet Power, as well as our apologies if we have not managed to do justice to all their insights.

We have been writing this book in England, during perhaps the most difficult period of our lives as a country. It has been a time when grounds for optimism have been in strictly limited supply. We do believe though that, in flipping schools, despite all the exasperation they sometimes cause us, and by doing this through real engagement with stakeholders, working from the inside out, we may be able to unlock one of the most important agents for positive change in society going forward.

That in itself, along with the creativity and passion we have witnessed in school leaders who understand the need to think and act differently, and who have the courage and strength of purpose to just get on and do it, is a very strong reason for us all still to be hopeful.

John West-Burnham

Malcolm Groves

September 2019

References

Abbott, L. and Nutbrown, C. (2001) *Experiencing Reggio Emilia: implications for pre-school provision*. Maidenhead: Open University Press.

Adamson, P. (2008) *The child care transition: a league table of early childhood education and care in economically advanced countries*. Florence: The United Nations Children's Fund.

Adey, P. and Dillon, J. (eds) (2012) *Bad education: debunking myths in education*. Maidenhead: Open University Press.

Ainsworth, M. S. and Bowlby, J. (1991) 'An ethological approach to personality development', *American Psychologist* 46 (4), pp.333–341.

Alexander, R. (ed) (2010) *Children, their world, their education: final report and recommendations of the Cambridge Primary Review*. Abingdon: Routledge.

Allen, G. (2011) *Early intervention: the next steps. An independent report to Her Majesty's Government*. London: The Stationery Office.

Andrews, J., Robinson, D. and Hutchinson, J. (2017) *Closing the gap? Trends in educational attainment and disadvantage*. London: Education Policy Institute.

Asbury, K. and Plomin, R. (2014) *G is for genes: the impact of genetics on education and achievement*. Chichester: John Wiley & Sons.

Audit Commission (2006) *More than the sum*. London: The Stationary Office.

Benn, M. (2018) *Life Lessons: the case for a national education service*. London: Verso.

Bergin, C. and Bergin, D. (2009) 'Attachment in the classroom', *Educational Psychology Review* 21 (2), pp.141–170.

Berry, W. (1992) *Sex, economy, freedom and community*. New York: Pantheon Books.

Biesta, G. J. (2010) 'Why "what works" still won't work: from evidence-based education to value-based education', *Studies in Philosophy and Education* 29 (5), pp.491–503.

Blakemore, S-J. (2019) *Inventing ourselves: the secret life of the teenage brain*. London: Black Swan.

Bodkin, J. (2019) 'Giving elderly hospital patients one extra meal a day cuts deaths by half, major NHS trial finds', *The Telegraph*, 12 January. Available at: https://www.telegraph.co.uk/news/2019/01/12/giving-elderlyhospital-patients-one-extra-meal-day-cuts-deaths/ (Accessed: 18 October 2019).

Bourdieu, P. (1986) 'The forms of capital' in Richardson, J. G. (ed), *Handbook of theory and research for the sociology of education*. New York: Greenwood Press, pp.241–258.

Bowers, A. P., Strelitz, J., Allen, J. and Donkin, A. (2012) *An equal start: improving outcomes in Children's Centres – the evidence review*. London: UCL Institute of Health Equity.

Brill, F., Grayson, H., Kuhn, L. and O'Donnell, S. (2018) *What impact does accountability have on curriculum, standards and engagement in education?* A literature review. Slough: National Foundation for Educational Research.

Byrne, L. (2008) 'Government plan to raise aspirations of millions of children.' Interview by Patrick Wintour and Allegra Stratton. *Guardian*, 15 December. Available at: https://www.theguardian.com/society/2008/dec/15/children-reform-service-society-government (Accessed: 16 October 2019).

Cambridge Public Schools (2017) *H415 leadership and community action*. Available at: https://secure2.cpsd.us/course_catalog/course_details.php?courseID=713 (Accessed 28 October 2019).

Capra, F. (2002) *The hidden connections: a science for sustainable living*. London: Harper Collins.

Chartered Institute of Personnel and Development (2019) *Executive pay in the FTSE 100: is everyone getting a fair slice of the cake?* Available at: http://highpaycentre.org/files/CIPD_HPC_FTSE_100_executive_pay_report.pdf (Accessed: 14 November 2019).

Christakis, N. and Fowler, J. (2011) *Connected: the surprising power of our social networks and how they shape our lives*. London: Harper Press.

Clahane, P. and M. Shields (2019) 'Great Yarmouth school a 'fourth emergency service', *BBC News*, 7 May. Available at: https://www.bbc.co.uk/news/uk-england-norfolk-48119099 (Accessed: 1 November 2019).

Claxton, G. and Lucas, B. (2015) *Educating Ruby*. Carmarthen: Crown House Publishing.

Constantino S. (2015) *Engage every family: five simple principles*. Thousand Oaks: Corwin.

Crehan, L. (2018) *Cleverlands: the secrets behind the success of the world's education superpowers*. London: Unbound.

Cunha, F., Heckman, J. J., Lochner, L. and Masterov, D. V. (2005) *Interpreting the evidence on life cycle skill formation*. Cambridge MA: National Bureau of Economic Research.

Day, C., Sammons, P., Hopkins, D., Harris, A., Leithwood, K., Gu, Q., Brown, E., Ahtaridou, E. and Kington, A. (2009) *The impact of school leadership on pupil outcomes*. Department for Children, Schools and Families. London: The Stationary Office.

Department for Education (2010) *The importance of teaching: the schools white paper 2010*. London: The Stationary Office.

Department for Education (2016) *Educational excellence everywhere*. London: The Stationary Office.

Department for Education (2017) *Statutory framework for the early years foundation stage: setting the standards for learning, development and care for children from birth to five*. London: The Stationary Office.

Department for Education (2018) *Schools, pupils and their characteristics: January 2018*. London: The Stationary Office.

Department for Education and Skills (2005) *Extended schools: access to opportunities and services for all*. London: The Stationary Office.

Desforges, C. and Abouchaar, A. (2003) *The impact of parental involvement, parental support and family education on pupil achievement and adjustment: a literature review*. Department for Education and Skills. London: The Stationary Office.

Diamond, J. (2005) *Collapse: how societies choose to fail or succeed*. London: Penguin.

Diamond, J. (2012) *The world until yesterday: what can we learn from traditional societies?* London: Allen Lane.

Diss, O. and Jarvie, M. (2016) *Unfinished business: where next for extended schools?* London: Child Poverty Action Group.

Drummond, M. J. (1991) 'The child and the primary curriculum – from policy to practice', *The Curriculum Journal* 2 (2).

Dunbar, R. (2010) *How many friends does one person need?* London: Faber & Faber.

Education Endowment Foundation (no date) *Teaching and learning toolkit: an accessible summary of the international evidence on teaching 5–16 year-olds*. Available at: https://educationendowmentfoundation.org.uk/evidence-summaries/teaching-learning-toolkit (Accessed: 6 November 2019).

Eells, R. J. (2011) 'Meta-analysis of the relationship between collective teacher efficacy and student achievement', *Dissertations* (133). Loyola eCommons.

ExpandED Schools (2013) *The 6000 Hour Learning Gap* [Video]. Available at: https://youtu.be/l8i4U-WWfho (Accessed: 21 October 2019).

Ferguson, D. and McIntyre, N. (2019) 'Revealed: how wealthy parents widen cash gap between state schools', *Guardian*, 14 July. Available at: https://www.theguardian.com/education/2019/jul/14/wealthy-parents-stoke-school-divide?CMP=share_btn_link (Accessed: 21 October 2019).

Fielding, M. (2000) 'The person-centred school', *Forum* 42 (2), pp.51–54.

Fielding, M. (2006) 'Leadership, radical student engagement and the necessity of person-centred education', *International Journal of Leadership in Education* 9 (4), pp.299–313.

Fielding, M. (2013) 'Still 'learning to be human': the radical educational legacy of John Macmurray', *Forum for promoting 3–19 comprehensive education* 55 (3), pp.461–472.

Fullan, M. (2010) *All systems go: the change imperative for whole system reform*. Thousand Oaks: Corwin Press.

Fullan, M. (2019a) 'The unity of the human race: our precarious future', *Education Weekly*, 25 August. Available at: http://blogs.edweek.org/edweek/finding_common_ground/2019/08/the_unity_of_the_human_race_our_precarious_future.html (Accessed: 7 November 2019).

Fullan, M. (2019b) 'Most examples of deep learning are not deep enough', *Education Weekly*, 28 August. Available at: http://blogs.edweek.org/edweek/finding_common_ground/2019/08/most_examples_of_deep_learning_are_not_deep_enough.html (Accessed: 7 November 2019).

Gallie, W. (1955) 'Essentially contested concepts', *Proceedings of the Aristotelian Society* 56 (1) pp.167–198.

Gardner, H. (1999) *Intelligence reframed: multiple intelligences for the 21st century*. New York: Basic Books.

Gawande, A. (2011) *The checklist manifesto: how to get things right*. London: Profile Books.

Gelsthorpe, T. and West-Burnham, J. (eds) (2003) *Educational leadership and the community: strategies for school improvement through community engagement*. London: Pearson Education.

Gilchrist, A. (2005) *The well-connected community: a networking approach to community development*. Bristol: Polity Press.

Gladwell, M. (2000) *The tipping point: how little things can make a big difference*. London: Abacus.

Goddard, R. D., Salloum, S. J. and Berebitsky, D. (2009) 'Trust as a mediator of the relationships between poverty, racial composition, and academic achievement: evidence from Michigan's public elementary schools', *Educational Administration Quarterly* 45 (2), pp.292–311.

Goldacre, B. (2013) *Building evidence into education*. Available at: http://media.education.gov.uk/assets/files/pdf/b/ben%20goldacre%20paper.pdf (Accessed: 31 October 2019).

Goodall, J. (2018) 'Parental engagement in children's learning: moving on from mass superstition', *Creative Education* 9 (11), pp.1611–1621.

Goodhart, D. (2017) *The road to somewhere: the populist revolt and the future of politics*. Oxford: Oxford University Press.

Goodman, P. (1964) *Compulsory miseducation*. New York: Horizon Press.

Gopnik, A. (2016) *The gardener and the carpenter: what the new science of child development tells us about the relationship between parents and children*. London: The Bodley Head.

Gorard, S. (2009) 'Serious doubts about school effectiveness', *British Educational Research Journal* 36 (5), pp.745–766.

Greany, T. and Higham, R. (2018) *Hierarchy, markets and networks: analysing the 'self-improving school-led system' agenda in England and the implications for schools*. London: UCL Institute of Education Press.

Grossman, R. and Leroux, C. (1996) 'A new Roseto effect: people are nourished by other people', *Chicago Tribune*, 11 October.

Groves, M., Hobbs, A. and Smith, C. (2015) *Shaping our futures: developing student-led research as a springboard for school transformation*. Schools of Tomorrow and SSAT. Available at: https://schoolsoftomorrow.org/wp-content/uploads/2018/11/Shaping-our-Futures-pages.pdf (Accessed: 30 October 2019).

Groves, M., Hobbs, A. and West-Burnham, J. (2017) *Leadership for tomorrow: beyond the school improvement horizon*. Carmarthen: Crown House Publishing.

Hands, C. (2010) 'Why collaborate? The differing reasons for secondary school educators' establishment of school-community partnerships', *School Effectiveness and School Improvement* 21 (2), pp.189–207.

Hargreaves, A. and Fullan, M. (2012) *Professional capital: transforming teaching in every school*. London: Routledge.

Hargreaves, D. (2012) *A self-improving school system: towards maturity*. Nottingham: National College for Teaching and Leadership.

Harper, R. and Kelly, M. (2003) *Measuring social capital in the United Kingdom*. London: Office for National Statistics.

Hart, B. and Risley, T. (2003) 'The early catastrophe: the 30 million word gap by age 3', *American Educator* 27 (1), pp.4–9.

Hart, R. (1992) *Children's participation: from tokenism to citizenship*. Florence: The United Nations Children's Fund.

Hart R. A. (2008) 'Stepping back from 'the ladder': reflections on a model of participatory work with children' in Reid A., Jensen B. B., Nikel J. and Simovska V. (eds) *Participation and learning: developing perspectives on education and the environment, health and sustainability.* Dordrecht: Springer.

Hattie, J. and Zierer, K. (2018) *10 mindframes for visible learning: teaching for success.* Abingdon: Routledge.

Holdsworth, R. (2011) 'Student action teams', *ASPRINworld* website. Available at: http://asprinworld.com/student_action_teams (Accessed: 30 October 2019).

Holt-Lunstad, J., Smith, T. B. and Layton, J. B. (2010) 'Social relationships and mortality risk: a meta-analytic review', *PLoS Medicine* 7 (7), e1000316.

House of Commons Education Committee (2019) *A ten-year plan for school and college funding.* London: The Stationary Office.

Hutchinson, J., Bonetti, S., Crenna-Jennings, W. and Akhal, A. (2019) *Education in England: annual report 2019.* London: Education Policy Institute.

Illich, I. (1970) *Deschooling society.* London: Marion Boyars.

Institute for Effective Education (2014) *What influences attainment at age 16? Best evidence in brief.* Available at: www.beib.org.uk

International Baccalaureate Organization (2016) *International Baccalaureate Middle Years Programme award.* Available at: https://www.ibo.org/globalassets/digital-tookit/brochures/1702-myp-brief-awards-en.pdf (Accessed: 28 October 2019).

IPPR Commission on Economic Justice (2018) *Propensity and justice: a plan for the new economy.* Available at: https://www.ippr.org/files/2018-08/1535639099_prosperity-and-justice-ippr-2018.pdf (Accessed: 21 October 2019).

Jerrim, J. and Shure, N. (2016) *Achievement of 15-year-olds in England: PISA 2015 national report.* Department for Education. London: The Stationary Office.

Joseph Rowntree Foundation (2018) *UK Poverty 2018.* Available at: https://www.jrf.org.uk/report/uk-poverty-2018 (Accessed: 18 October 2019).

Klinenberg, E. (2018) *Palaces for the people: how to build a more equal and united society.* London: The Bodley Head.

Lasker, R. D., Weiss, E. S., and Miller, R. (2001) 'Partnership synergy: a practical framework for studying and strengthening the collaborative advantage', *The Millbank Quarterly* 79 (2), pp. 179–205.

Law, S. (2006) *The war for children's minds.* Abingdon: Routledge.

Leadbeater, C. (2004) *Personalisation through participation: a new script for public services.* London: Demos.

Linsky, M. and Lawrence, J. (2011) 'Adaptive challenges for school leadership' in O'Sullivan, H. and West-Burnham, J. (eds) *Leading and managing schools.* London: SAGE Publications.

Maak, T. (2007) 'Responsible leadership, stakeholder engagement, and the emergence of social capital', *Journal of Business Ethics* 74 (4), pp.329–343.

MacAskill, W. (2015) *Doing good better: effective altruism and a radical new way to make a difference.* London: Guardian Faber Publishing.

Macleod, S., Sharp, C., Bernardinelli, D., Skipp, A. and Higgins, S. (2015) *Supporting the attainment of disadvantaged pupils: articulating success and good practice.* Department for Education. London: The Stationary Office.

Macmurray, J. (1933) *Interpreting the universe.* London: Faber & Faber.

Manchanda, R. (2014) *What makes us sick? Look upstream* [Video]. Available at: https://www.ted.com/talks/rishi_manchanda_what_makes_us_get_sick_look_upstream?language=en (Accessed: 18 October 2019).

Mann, A., Kashefpakdel, E. T., Rehill, J. and Huddleston, P. (2017) *Contemporary transitions: young Britons reflect on life after school and college.* London: Education and Employers.

Mann, A., Rehill, J. and Kashefpakdel, E. T. (2018) *Employer engagement in education: insights from international evidence for effective practice and future research.* London: Education and Employers.

Maslow, A. H. (1943) 'A theory of human motivation', *Psychological Review* 50 (4), pp.370–396.

Minogue, O. and Moore, A. (2013) *Too young to fail: closing the education achievement gap in Northern Ireland.* London: Save the Children UK.

Monbiot, G. (2018) 'The town that's found a potential cure for illness – community', *Guardian*, 21 February. Available at: https://www.theguardian.com/commentisfree/2018/feb/21/town-cure-illness-community-frome-somerset-isolation (Accessed: 18 October 2019).

Moreno, M., Mulford, B. and Hargreaves, A. (2007) *Trusting leadership: from standards to social capital.* Nottingham: National College for School Leadership.

Morrell, D. (1973) *Community Schools Gazette*

Morris, H. (1924) *The village college: being a memorandum on the provision of education and social facilities for the countryside, with special reference to Cambridgeshire.*

Moullin, S., Waldfogel, J. and Washbrook, E. (2014) *Baby bonds: parenting, attachment and a secure base for children.* London: The Sutton Trust.

Muijs, D. (2010) 'Effectiveness and disadvantage in education: can a focus on effectiveness aid equity in education?' in Raffo, C., Dyson, A., Gunter, H., Hall, D., Jones L. and Kalambouka A. (eds), *Education and poverty in affluent countries.* Abingdon: Routledge, pp.85–96.

Noddings, N. (1992) *The challenge to care in schools: an alternative approach to education.* New York: Teachers College Press.

Nguyen, T. (2014) 'Success starts with self-mastery: 7 effective strategies', *SKIPPRICHARD* website. Available at: https://www.skipprichard.com/success-starts-with-self-mastery-7-effective-strategies/ (Accessed: 14 November 2019).

OCED (2015) *Education at a glance 2015: OECD indicators.* Paris: OECD Publishing.

OECD (2018) *Equity in education: breaking down barriers to social mobility.* Paris: OECD Publishing.

Ofsted (2018) *Maintained schools and academies inspections and outcomes as at 31 December 2017.* London: The Stationary Office.

Pentland, A. (2014) *Social physics: how good ideas spread – the lessons from a new science.* Brunswick Victoria: Scribe Publications.

Pinker, S. (2014) *The village effect: why face-to-face contact matters.* London: Atlantic Books.

Plomin, R. (2018) *Blueprint: how DNA makes us who we are.* London: Allen Lane.

Pont, B., Nusche, D. and Hopkins, D. (2008) *Improving school leadership. Volume 2: case studies on system leadership.* Paris: OECD Publishing.

Prime Minister's Strategy Unit (2006) *The UK government's approach to public service reform.* London: The Stationary Office.

Putnam, R. (2000) *Bowling alone: the collapse and revival of American community.* New York: Simon & Schuster.

Putnam, R. D. and Feldstein, L. (2003) *Better together: restoring the American community.* New York: Simon & Schuster.

Quigley, A., Muijs, D. and Stringer, E. (2018) *Metacognition and self-regulated learning: guidance report.* London: Education Endowment Foundation.

Raikes, H. (1993) 'Relationship duration in infant care: time with a high-ability teacher and infant-teacher attachment', *Early Childhood Research Quarterly* 8 (3), pp.309–325.

Rajan, R. (2019) *The third pillar: the revival of community in a polarised world.* London: William Collins.

Ringelmann, M. (1913) 'Research on animate sources of power: the work of man', *Annales de l'Institut National Agronomique* 12 (2), pp.1–40.

Rose, N. (2017) 'Putting evidence to work', *Evidence into practice: a blog about evidence-informed teaching*, 21 October. Available at: https://evidenceintopractice.wordpress.com (Accessed: 25 October 2019).

Sackett, D. L., Rosenberg, W. M., Gray, J. M., Haynes, R. B. and Richardson, W. S. (1996) 'Evidence based medicine: what it is and what it isn't', *British Medical Journal* 312, pp.71–72.

Sahlberg, P. (2011) *Finnish lessons: what can the world learn from educational change in Finland?* New York: Teachers College Press.

Savage, M., Devine, F., Cunningham, N., Taylor, M., Li, Y., Hjellbrekke, J., Le Roux, B., Friedman, S. and Miles, A. (2013) 'A new model of social class? Findings from the BBC's Great British class survey experiment', *Sociology* 47 (2), pp.219–250.

Seifter, H. (2001) *Leadership ensemble: lessons in collaborative management from the world's only conductorless orchestra*. New York: Times Books.

Sergiovanni, T. J. (1992) *Moral leadership: getting to the heart of school improvement*. San Francisco: Jossey-Bass.

Sikora J., Evans, M. D. R. and Kelley, J. (2018) 'Scholarly culture: how books in adolescence enhance adult literacy, numeracy and technology skills in 31 societies', *Social Science Research* 77, pp.1–15.

Silins, H. and Mulford, B. (2002) 'Leadership and school results' in Leithwood, K. and Hallinger, P. (eds) *Second international handbook of educational leadership and administration*. Norwell MA: Kluwer Academic Press, pp.561–612.

Singer, P. (2015) *The most good you can do: how effective altruism is changing ideas about living ethically*. New Haven: Yale University Press.

Standing, G. (2011) *The precariat: the new dangerous class*. London: Bloomsbury.

Strand, S. (2016) 'Do some schools narrow the gap? Differential school effectiveness revisited', *Review of Education* 4 (2), pp.107–144.

The Children's Society (2019) *What are the effects of child poverty?* Available at: https://www.childrenssociety.org.uk/what-we-do/our-work/ending-child-poverty/what-are-the-effects-of-child-poverty (Accessed: 21 October 2019).

The Edge Foundation (2019) *Edge Future learning: our principles for deeper learning*. Available at: https://www.edge.co.uk/sites/default/files/documents/future_learning_handbook_final_-_web.pdf (Accessed: 30 October 2019).

The Sutton Trust and the Social Mobility Commission (2019) *Elitist Britain 2019: the educational backgrounds of Britain's leading people*. Available at: www.suttontrust.com/research-paper/elitist-britain-2019 (Accessed: 18 October 2019).

Timpson website. Available at: https://www.timpson.co.uk (Accessed: 17 October 2019).

United Nations (no date) 'Sustainable development goal 4', *Sustainable Development Goals Knowledge Platform*. Available at: https://sustainabledevelopment.un.org/sdg4 (Accessed: 1 November 2019).

Verkaik, R. (2018) *Posh boys: how English public schools ruin Britain*. London: Oneworld Publications.

Wenger, E. (1998) 'Communities of practice: learning as a social system', *The Systems Thinker* 9 (5), pp.2–3.

Wilkinson, D., Bryson, A. and Stokes, L. (2018) 'How much do schools matter?', *National Institute of Economic and Social Research* website, 4 February. Available at: https://www.niesr.ac.uk/blog/how-much-do-schools-matter (Accessed: 17 October 2019).

Wilkinson, R. and Pickett, K. (2010) *The spirit level: why equality is better for everyone*. London: Penguin.

Williams, J. (2019) *What do we want from the next Prime Minister? Policy ideas for new leadership: education*. London: Policy Exchange.

Williams, K., Papadopoulou V. and Booth N. (2012) *Prisoners' childhood and family backgrounds: results from the Surveying Prisoner Crime Reduction (SPCR) longitudinal cohort study of prisoners*. London: Ministry of Justice.

Wilshaw, M. (2016) Speech to FASNA Autumn Conference, 2 November. Available at: https://www.gov.uk/government/speeches/sir-michael-wilshaws-speech-at-the-fasna-autumn-conference (Accessed: 4 November 2019).

Wilson, D. S. (2019) *This view of life: completing Darwinian evolution*. New York: Pantheon.

Wolf, S. and Bruhn, J. (1993) *The power of clan: the influence of human relationships on heart disease*. New Jersey: Transaction Publishers.

Index

F

G

H

I

J

L

T

U

V

W

Praise for Flipping Schools!

"It is rare to find, in a field as crowded as education, innovative thinking that is both out-of-the-box and yet realistic, so as to be eminently actionable.

"If education is to impart not only knowledge, but also skills and character, it is clear that one's family and societal environments play a huge role; we all know that 'it takes a village': education, more exactly learning, significantly happens outside formal classrooms; a child's environment has enormous impact on expectations, self-confidence, resilience, and many other competencies.

"By shining the spotlight on the critical social factors adjacent to formal education, the authors force the conversation to expand its purview, in a refreshingly original and useful direction."

Charles Fadel, Founder, Center for Curriculum Redesign and author of *Four-Dimensional Education* **and** *Artificial Intelligence in Education*

"This timely book challenges our thinking about the purpose of schools, giving us a radical critique of the current 'school effectiveness' paradigm in England. Deeply human in its approach, it asks the big questions and gives us some ways forward."

Steve Munby, International education consultant. Formerly chief executive of the National College for School Leadership in England and of the Education Development Trust

"As an educator, I have always held the African proverb that 'it takes a village to raise a child' close to my heart and this wonderful books not only explains why but exemplifies how."

Richard Gerver, award-winning speaker, bestselling author, world-renowned thinker and former primary headteacher

"This is an incisive book about what we need to do to make schooling fit for purpose. It describes where we are, unpicks how we got here and charts some vital steps forward for individuals and communities. It's a flipping good book about schooling."

Professor Mick Waters, formerly Director of Curriculum for the Qualifications and Curriculum Authority, Chief Education Officer in Manchester, and headteacher in Cumbria

"Flipping Schools is an immensely important and timely book written with humility and a passionate commitment to providing future generations with the preparation for life they deserve.

"This meticulously researched work, packed with practical examples and useful tools, reaches the heart of the reasons why our education system can no longer address the pressing needs of England's 21st century society without refocusing priorities.

"The case for a fundamental rethink of the prevailing models of accountability and leadership and the social factors that are holding it back is compelling. I cannot recommend it strongly enough to every senior leadership team and policymaker."

Brian Lightman, Education consultant and former General Secretary of the Association of School and College Leaders

"This is a thoughtful and challenging book that deals with the challenges of developing the school system in England. To have a school led system, schools need to be at the heart of their community and school leaders need to have the courage and confidence to do what is right for the young people in their care. West-Burnham and Groves present thought provoking views on the way forward. A must-read for aspiring and current school leaders."

Sue Williamson, Chief Executive, SSAT